GUY PÈNE DU BOIS

Guy Pène du Bois

PAINTER OF MODERN LIFE

by Betsy Fahlman

THE QUANTUCK LANE PRESS

NEW YORK

Guy Pène du Bois: Painter of Modern Life

by Betsy Fahlman

Copyright © 2004 by James Graham & Sons, Inc.
All works by Guy Pène du Bois copyright © The Estate of Yvonne Pène du Bois McKenney

The text of this book is composed in Bodoni Old Face (Adobe) and FF Seria Sans (FontShop)
With the display set in Acanthus (FontShop)
Design and composition by John Bernstein Design, Inc.
Manufacturing by Mondadori Printing, Verona

Library of Congress Cataloging-in-Publication Data

Fahlman, Betsy.
Guy Pene Du Bois / Betsy Fahlman.
    p.   cm.

Includes bibliographical references and index.
ISBN 1-59372-005-X

1. Du Bois, Guy Pène, 1884–1958—Catalogs. I. Du Bois, Guy Pène, 1884–1958. II. Title.
ND237.D75A4 2004
759.13—dc22   2004001899

The Quantuck Lane Press, New York

Distributed by:
W.W. Norton & Company
500 Fifth Avenue, New York, NY 10110
www.wwnorton.com

W.W. Norton & Company Ltd.
Castle House, 75/76 Wells Street, London, W1T 3QT

1 2 3 4 5 6 7 8 9 0

Frontispiece: **Photograph of Guy Pène du Bois**, 1930s
Archive photograph courtesy of Kraushaar Galleries, New York

Contents

Acknowledgments

Ames Graham & Sons, Inc. has represented the work of Guy Pène du Bois since 1960. In that capacity the gallery has organized a number of significant exhibitions. The first, in 1961, featured thirty important paintings and drawings, including *Race Track*, *Longchamps*, *The Doll and the Monster*, and *Balloon Woman, Forest of Rambouillet*. Two years later the gallery mounted "Paintings of Twenty Younger Years 1913–1933." Over the next quarter of a century, James Graham & Sons held three shows devoted to the artist: one in 1970; another in 1979, titled "Guy Pène du Bois: Painter, Draftsman and Critic"; and in 1983, an exhibition that featured portraits of Mura Dehn and Portia Lebrun. The gallery also presented the 1998 exhibition "Guy Pène du Bois: Returning to America," and, in 2000, the only one to date devoted to the artist's works on paper.

For this current exhibition, "Guy Pène du Bois: Painter of Modern Life," James Graham & Sons is delighted to work again with American art scholar Betsy Fahlman. Our relationship with Betsy dates back to the gallery's 1998 Pène du Bois show, for which she wrote the accompanying catalogue essay about the artist's later compositions. However, Betsy's interest in the artist dates back much further, to 1973, when she was an undergraduate at Mount Holyoke College. She later chose Pène du Bois as the subject of her dissertation at the University of Delaware. Betsy's doctoral research developed into *Guy Pène du Bois: Artist about Town*, the 1980 exhibition and catalogue produced by the Corcoran Gallery of Art in Washington, D.C. Betsy's scholarship continued when, in 1995, she curated "Imaging the Twenties: The Work of Guy Pène du Bois," which was held at the Sordoni Art Gallery at Wilkes University, Wilkes-Barre, Pennsylvania, and wrote the essay for the accompanying catalogue.

Guy Pène du Bois: Painter of Modern Life, also the result of Betsy's careful research, is the most comprehensive book on the artist's life and work to date. Betsy's essay sheds new light on an artist who has been aptly characterized as "the satirist of the well-fed classes."* Her thoughtful essay references many primary documents, including the Guy Pène du Bois Papers and the Kraushaar Papers, both in the collection of the Archives of American Art, as well as Pène du Bois's diary and many of the articles he published as a reporter. The correspondence between Pène du Bois and John Kraushaar, the artist's dealer during his lifetime, is fascinating, and closely documents the struggles Pène du Bois faced both in America and abroad. We are indebted to Betsy for her scholarship and enthusiasm.

Many individuals and institutions have made important contributions to this project, in particular: The Art Institute of Chicago (Matthew Cook); The Barnes Foundation (Renee Bomgardner); John Bernstein; Berry-Hill Galleries (Bruce Weber); Brooklyn Museum of Art (Linda Ferber); Carey Ellis Company (Amy Munger); The Corcoran Museum of Art (Nancy Swallow); Curtis Galleries (Jenny Sponberg); Delaware Art Museum (Sarena Deglin); The Detroit Institute of Arts (Sylvia Inwood); The Estate of Yvonne Pène du Bois McKenney; Hirshhorn Museum and Sculpture Garden (Amy Densford, Brian Kavanagh); Hunter Museum of American Art (Elizabeth Le); Mr. and Mrs. Iannone; Indianapolis Museum of Art (Ruth Roberts); James Graham & Sons, Inc. (Robert C. Graham, Jr., Cameron M. Shay, Katie Clifford, Carrie Hart, Courtney Hinman, Terin Lokey); Kraushaar Galleries (Katherine Degn, Carolyn Pastel, Carole Pesner); Lehigh University Art Galleries (Ricardo Viera); Los Angeles County Museum of Art (Giselle Arteaga-Johnson); The Metropolitan Museum of Art (Ida Balboul, Minora Collins, Barbara Weinberg); Museum of Modern Art (Mikki Carpenter); The Naples Museum of Art (Liz Hamilton); National Gallery of Art (Peter Huestis); National Portrait Gallery (Kristin Smith); New Britain Museum of American Art (Mary Ellen Ellis, Douglas Hyland); The Newark Museum (Scott Hankins); Michael Owen; Quantuck Lane Press (James L. Mairs, Brook Wilensky-Lanford); Martha Parrish; Jim Reinish; Ringling Museum of Art (Heidi Taylor); Nancy Rosen; The Smart Museum of Art (Jennifer Moyer); Sordoni Art Gallery (Karen Evans Kaufer); Lois Wagner; Weatherspoon Art Museum (Maggie Gregory); Weston, Patrick, Willard & Redding (Michael Wiggins); Whitney Museum of American Art (Barbara Haskell, Barbi Spieler); and all the private collectors who have so generously lent their paintings to the exhibition. We are forever grateful.

Priscilla Vail Caldwell
Director, James Graham & Sons, Inc.

---

*Catherine Beach Ely, in *Guy Pène du Bois 1884–1958*, exh. cat. (New York: James Graham & Sons, March 17–April 15, 1961).

6

A scholar accumulates many debts throughout the process of research and writing, and I gratefully acknowledge the assistance of Kay Arthur, Sara Bearss, Avis Berman, Barry Downes, Don Gunter, Jeffrey Hayes, Gail Levin, Bob Lucas, Mary Meade, Jocelyn Moralde, Mary C. Pontillo, Pam Scott, Susan Selkirk, and Pierre L. Ullman. My husband, Daniel Ball, is always supportive of my projects, and I am deeply grateful for his contributions great and small to my work.

Staff members at museums and institutions have been most helpful and I particularly would like to thank those who assisted me at the Amon Carter Museum (Rick Stewart), the Art Students League (Stephanie Cassidy), the Barnes Foundation (Renee Bomgardner, Katy Rawdon-Faucett), the Brooklyn Museum of Art (Linda Ferber), the Corcoran Gallery of Art (Kelly O'Neil Baker), the Hirshhorn Museum and Sculpture Garden (Amy Densford, Judith Zilczer), the Indianapolis Museum of Art (Harriet Warkel), the Joslyn Art Museum (Janet Farber), the Naples Museum of Art (Jessica M. Wozniak), the National Academy of Design (Marshall Price, Paula Pineda), the National Gallery of Art (Anne Halpern, Carlotta Owens, Alicia B. Thomas), the Newark Museum (Jeffrey V. Moy), the Newark Public Library (William J. Dane), the Parrish Art Museum (Novella Laspia), the Parsons School of Design (X. Theodore Barber), the Passaic County Historical Society (Betty Lou Walker), the Passaic Public Library (Jean Ellis), the Philadelphia Museum of Art (Jane Joe, Sarah Powers), the Princeton University Library (Margaret Rich), Smithsonian American Art Museum (Andrew L. Thomas, Peter A. Juley and Son Collection), Smithsonian Institution (Dave Burgevin), the South Orange Public Library (Ellen Columbus), the University of Virginia Art Museum (Suzanne Foley), the Wichita Art Museum (Stephen Gleissner), and the Whitney Museum of American Art (Anita Duquette).

For their many kindnesses, I am very thankful for the help given me by staff members at several galleries, including Bruce Weber (Berry-Hill Galleries), Janis Conner and Joel Rosenkranz (Conner-Rosenkranz), M.P. Naud (Hirschl & Adler Galleries), Katherine Degn (Kraushaar Galleries), and Michael Owen (Owen Gallery).

1

The resources of the Archives of American Art, the Amon Carter Museum library, the Beinecke Library, the National Archives, and the Smithsonian American Art Museum/National Portrait Gallery Library have proved invaluable.

I am most grateful for the generosity of the Estate of Yvonne Pène du Bois McKenney.

It has been a real pleasure to work with the staff at James Graham & Sons. Priscilla Vail Caldwell first suggested the project and has been enthusiastic from its inception. This would never have been realized without her hard work and support. I would like to thank Robert C. Graham, Jr., Cameron M. Shay, Carrie Hart, Courtney Hinman, Katie Clifford, and Terin Lokey as well. I am also grateful for the exceptional professional skills of designer John Bernstein and copy editor Mary Gladue, who have been magicians in transforming my manuscript into this handsome book.

Betsy Fahlman
Arizona State University

7

FIG. 1: **Cirque d'Hiver, Paris** | 1926, watercolor and graphite on paper, 9¼ x 15⅞ inches

Signed and dated at lower left: Guy Pène du Bois Paris 1926 | titled verso: Cirque d'Hiver

James Graham & Sons, Inc., New York

Painter of Modern Life

INTRODUCTION | Guy Pène du Bois (1884–1958; frontispiece), one of America's most stylish painters in the second quarter of the twentieth century, keenly observed the spectacle of social theater he saw around him and deftly captured the sophisticated spirit of the era in which he worked. Drawing his inspiration from the life he knew — a lesson he had learned early in his career from his teacher Robert Henri — Guy found his distinctive vision in the lively portrayal of human interaction. The uneasy relations between men and women particularly interested him, and he often composed his subjects in pairs within a metropolitan environment, contrasting their highly structured roles as though parts in a play. His sharply urbane perspective enabled him to record his figures with considerable wit, as he delineated their foibles and pretensions, which were often dictated by a combination of class, profession, and gender. An artful stylist who was more interested in types than individuals, Guy possessed considerable technical skill that enabled him to create images strongly imbued with the flavor of his time.

Pène du Bois remains an important figure whose career embraced the professions of artist, writer-critic, and teacher. As a critic, he was one of the most articulate explicators of the tradition of urban realism established by The Eight, with whose leader he studied. In artistic style, he was a progressive realist rather than an avant-garde modernist. The central formal elements of his work were summarized by sculptor Mahonri Young: "His form is sound, his composition very individual, and his color rich and very personal."[1]

His titles often convey the contrasts he found so intriguing — *Amateur and Professional* (1912, unlocated), *Ancient and Modern Styles* (1929, unlocated), and *Mr. and Mrs. Middleclass* (1936, fig. 42) — and he commonly executed paintings of paired figures — as with *Blonde and Brunette* (1915, p. 87), *Father and Son* (1929, p. 117), and *Mother and Daughter* (1928, p. 118; all Whitney Museum of American Art). He conceived his figures as mannequins over whom he draped the costumes of their privileged roles.

Pène du Bois participates in a long tradition of social observation that was the hallmark of nineteenth-century French artists Honoré Daumier, Jean-Louis Forain, T. A. Steinlen, Constantin Guys, and Edgar Degas, yet he remained grounded in his native country. As Mahonri Young observed in 1921, "But though his outlook is French, it is American French."[2] Collector Duncan Phillips concurred:

> Du Bois is to New York what Forain is to Paris, but his wit is less caustic and his weapon blunt by comparison. Whereas Forain is passionately concerned about the immolation of the victims of lust and war, du Bois avoids drama and grimness and tolerates the wicked world with a shrug and a smile, seldom revealing the strong emotions which are often the starting point for the satirist's angst and scorn.[3]

8

His renderings of the "mannered dance of social discourse"[4] are reminiscent of the stylized sculptures of Elie Nadelman, another artist with élan. With a wit both casual and elegant, Pène du Bois presents a *comédie humaine* of social manners with ironic detachment, as "an amused spectator of the passing show, painting the smart foibles of the Gotham world."[5] The French spirit imbued his outlook and work, but he never regarded himself as anything other than American. In an era in which issues of cultural nationalism were prominent in contemporary intellectual discourse, he never felt sufficiently estranged from the country of his birth to desire to become an expatriate.

Guy Pène du Bois has long been curiously invisible within the history of American art. That he has remained somewhat below the scholarly radar is the result of how his career played out — what he most wanted to do was paint, but he needed to write in order to support his painting. He was an excellent and insightful critic, yet the effort often drained his energies for the studio, as did his many years of teaching. His work is surprisingly well represented in American museums — a fact due more to generous private donations than to institutional decisions to purchase — but it has been the rare museum that hangs his work and gives it proper interpretation. Pène du Bois is not identified with a major movement but rather is part of a broader artistic trend in representational styles and figure painting. Though harder to categorize, his sheer strength as an artist shows that he deserves far greater prominence in the history of American art than he has been given.

EARLY YEARS | Born in Brooklyn in 1884, Guy was the son of journalist, writer, and bibliophile Henri Pène du Bois, whose Creole family roots were in Louisiana. Guy's lifelong admiration for Gallic culture was established early. Henri had a passion for French literature and named his son after his friend Guy de Maupassant — considered by many to be the greatest French short-story writer — and in his early years Guy spoke only French. An aristocratic and impractical man of letters, Henri's French sympathies made a deep impression on his son, but Guy soon came to realize that he and his father had little in common, at least in terms of fundamental art values. Whereas Henri favored fin-de-siècle literary modes, his son was solidly aligned with the realism of modern America.

Guy grew up in several New York boroughs, including Staten Island, where his family moved in 1898. In 1899 he enrolled in the New York School of Art and his first teacher was the institution's founder, painter William Merritt Chase. Always fashionably dressed and bit of a dandy, Chase presented his critiques with great theatricality and made a strong impression on those enrolled in his classes. Guy and his fellow students began their training with drawing after the nude, and, when sufficiently skilled, advanced to making oil sketches. Chase taught

9

them a painterly technique and exposed them to the realist work of old masters and contemporary academic artists. Although his fundamental philosophy was grounded in a Whistlerian art-for-art's-sake, Chase's assured and fluid realism was much admired by his students. (Later, after Guy studied with the legendary and charismatic teacher-painter Robert Henri, he would judge his first teacher facile and superficial, but it was Chase who first showed his students that a life in art was possible.[6])

Life in the Life Class: Studies with Robert Henri

Robert Henri began teaching at the New York School of Art during the 1902–3 term, and Guy Pène du Bois found himself in a stimulating and heady classroom environment. He and his classmates learned to be men first and artists second, and to be inspired in their art by the life they knew around them. Henri electrified his classes and stirred his students' imaginations. As Guy recalled, "Henri set the class in an uproar."[7]

Whether or not the students recognized how truly revolutionary their teacher was, they certainly understood that his approach to art and his manner of teaching were different from anything they had experienced. From him they learned to value both the "quality of the paint" and the "quality of the subject."[8] There was less talk of brushwork than there had been in Chase's classes, as Henri "emphasized an interpretation of life rather than an exposition of virtuosity."[9] He urged his students: "Everything in life is a subject, but it is not the subject that counts; it is what you yourself bring to it."[10] His lectures were magnetic and his advice

FIG. 2: **Robert Henri's Afternoon Life Class, New York School of Art**, 1903–4, Henri is seated in the front row; at center, to the right of him, is Guy Pène du Bois.

Archive photograph courtesy of Whitney Museum of American Art, New York

---

FIG. 3: EDWARD HOPPER (American, 1882–1967)

Portrait of Guy Pène du Bois, ca. 1904, oil on canvas, 24⅜ x 17 inches
Signed at lower left: Edward Hopper

Bernard Goldberg Fine Arts, LLC, New York

FIG. 4: **Portrait of a Man**, ca. 1904, oil on panel, 12¼ x 9¼ inches
Signed at lower right: Sketch by Du Bois

Private collection

FIG. 5: **Patrick Henry Bruce**, 1904, oil on canvas, 40 x 32½ inches
Signed and dated at lower left: Guy Pène du Bois '04

National Portrait Gallery, Smithsonian Institution, Washington, D.C.

3   4   5

inspiring, though he did not encourage his students to imitate him. Henri's ideas had the effect of revelation—"Life certainly did that day stride into the life class"[11]—and his precepts remained fundamental to Guy's philosophy as an artist and as a critic.

In Henri's classes, students learned that technique was merely a tool, not the end goal. Quick oil sketches were painted, without preliminary drawings, directly on canvas with large brushes, and the careful drawings Guy had produced for his other teachers were replaced with compositions of bold, vigorous strokes.

Guy did well enough in his studies to be appointed his teacher's assistant in one of the classes, and he also sold his first painting, a portrait of a Staten Island resident. Some of his fellow students—several of whom became well known—can be seen in a 1903–4 photograph of Henri's "Afternoon Life Class" at the New York School of Art (fig. 2). Among them are Edward Hopper, who remained a lifelong friend, Clarence K. Chatterton, Arthur E. Cedarquist, Glenn O. Coleman, Rockwell Kent, Walter Biggs, Gifford Beal, George Bellows, Homer Boss, Patrick Henry Bruce, Oliver N. Chaffee, Lawrence Dresser, Arnold Friedman, Julius Golz, Jr., Prosper Invernizzi, Edward Keefe, John Koopman, Vachel Lindsay, Walter Pach, Eugene Speicher, Carl Sprinchorn, Walter Tittle, and Clifton Webb. The enduring personal bonds forged in Henri's classroom reinforced what would become Guy's lifelong commitment to realism.

Portraits were common early subjects, and Guy and his classmates often painted likenesses of each other—young, ambitious artists at the beginning of their careers. Edward Hopper made an oil sketch of Guy (fig. 3), who likewise painted an unknown man from his class (fig. 4) and one of Patrick Henry Bruce (fig. 5). Darkly brushed and somewhat moody in atmosphere, these portraits convey the serious image of the mature artists the students aimed to be one day.

11

Chase was more of a showman than Henri, but both were riveting teachers, urging their students to study the great realists of the past: seventeenth-century Dutch painters Rembrandt and Frans Hals and Spaniard Diego Velázquez; nineteenth-century French artists Daumier, Gustave Courbet, Jean-François Millet, Édouard Manet, and Degas; and contemporary academics such as Jean-Léon Gérôme. Henri, who had lived in France between 1888 and 1891, encouraged them to read works by French authors, undoubtedly reinforcing the strong French orientation Guy had already gained from his upbringing.

Although he would eventually come to disagree with Henri on some issues, Guy's admiration of his teacher was steadfast; as he asserted in 1920, "You know that in any case if I have sometimes not liked the work I have always loved the man."[12]

6

An Art Student in Paris

In April 1905 Guy traveled to Europe with his father, who had been sent by the *New York American* to review exhibitions. After a few weeks in London, mostly spent visiting museums, they settled in Paris, the destination of choice for an international array of art students. His father was busy during the day and traveled regularly, leaving Guy on his own. They stayed at a small hotel; an early oil likely records one of its rooms, or perhaps one from the hotel in Brittany at which he lodged on a visit to the coast (p. 71). In any event, the furnishings do not resemble any seen in his later Staten Island interiors and the size of the work is typical of his French paintings.

Guy enrolled for a short time in the popular Atelier Colarossi and also took private lessons from Théophile Steinlen. He reveled in the life of an art student, and enjoyed meeting new artists (and the writers he met through his father) and seeing other Americans. His experiences in Robert Henri's class had prepared him to take advantage of Paris, a city that proved to be his most influential teacher. He haunted the museums and galleries and began to pursue themes that would interest him throughout his career. He sat for hours in cafés with his sketchbook, honing his observational skills as he studied people and the nuances of their social interactions. Although in France he was largely self-educated, his years of study in New York meant he was skilled enough to make his exhibition debut at the Paris Salon in 1905.

7

FIG. 6: **Artist's Studio**, 1905,
ink on paper, 9 x 11¾ inches
Signed and dated lower right:
   Guy Pène du Bois '05

Unlocated; Archive photograph courtesy of
the Estate of Yvonne Pène du Bois McKenney

FIG. 7: **War**, ca. 1905–6,
charcoal on paper, 11¾ x 8⅞ inches
Titled at bottom center: WAR.

The Estate of Yvonne Pène du Bois McKenney
and James Graham & Sons, Inc., New York

12

The body of work he produced in Paris reflects the strong impact French artists such as Toulouse-Lautrec, Daumier, Degas, Forain, and Steinlen had on him, and is infused with the French spirit. He found his subjects at cafés and cabarets, at the opera, in the public gardens — anywhere people gathered. Social exchanges, particularly between men and women, fascinated him, and the artist proved to be a sharp observer of contemporary life, positioning himself within a long tradition of aesthetic boulevardiers.

Guy's drawings show a broad range of themes. Some present a stereotypical image of a young painter's plight, as in *Artist's Studio* (1905, fig. 6), which portrays a scene right out of Puccini's romantically tragic opera *La Bohème*. A semi-clad model offers comfort to the discouraged artist sitting slumped in a chair. Inspiration — as well as, perhaps, his manly powers — appears to have deserted him. Guy had taken a small studio on the rue de la Grande Chaumière, a neighborhood popular with artists. Such a scene could have been emblematic of his own experience. *Street Corner* (1905, private collection) depicts an impending liaison between a man in a bowler hat and a woman holding a muff. Many of these early sketches, executed in pen and ink, are characterized by a thin, nervous line and are very continental in theme. Some, such as his allegorical figure *War* (ca. 1905–6, fig. 7), appear to be classroom assignments, whereas the narrative content of others suggests a literary inspiration. A dramatic image, *Rue des Écoles* (1905, fig. 8), for example, is inscribed "Je suis royaliste!

FIG. 8: **Rue des Écoles**, 1905, graphite on paper, 11¼ x 9 inches
Dated at lower right: 05
Inscribed at bottom:
    Je suis royaliste! Mais! Mon /
    Royaume n'est pas de ce / monde

The Estate of Yvonne Pène du Bois McKenney and James Graham & Sons, Inc., New York

FIG. 9: **Untitled (Man in Overcoat with Suitcase)**, ca. 1905–6, ink and pencil on paper, 11¾ x 8⅞ inches
Unsigned

Bernard Goldberg Fine Arts, LLC, New York

13

8

9

Mais! Mon Royaume n'est pas de ce monde!" ("I am a royalist! But! My kingdom is not of this world!") It does not appear to have been sketched from life, although the story from which it is derived is unknown. The old-fashioned clothing style in *Untitled (Man in Overcoat with Suitcase)* (ca. 1905–6, fig. 9) also suggests a source that was not directly observed.

Guy's strengths as an artist are first revealed in his paintings from this period. Although a student of the leader of The Eight, his earliest work predates their landmark exhibition of 1908 at the Macbeth Gallery and continued to parallel their work in theme and style throughout the teens. In Paris he executed his first independent paintings, some of which — *Paris Street Scene* (ca. 1905, p. 70) is one — document his exploration of the city.[13] Other works record the relaxed sexual atmosphere long associated with artist life in Paris. His risqué *Lady in Bed* (1905, p. 69) has much in common with John Sloan's *The Cot* (1907, Bowdoin College Museum of Art), and also resembles *Nude Crawling into Bed* (ca. 1903–5, Whitney Museum of American Art), a piece done by his friend Edward Hopper. Nevertheless, Guy draws on historical French tradition in his depictions of such scenes. He did a number of sketches for *Lady in Bed*, including *Untitled (Woman Curled Up in Bed)* (ca. 1905, fig. 11). The woman depicted in the sketch and painting could well be the one who puts on her black stockings in another small dark work (p. 68). A bed is visible in the background at left and her clothes are piled carelessly on the floor beside her. The furnishings are sparse, and the brown tonalities that dominate the painting reinforce the ordinariness of the room. The tiny windows near the ceiling suggest a basement location. A pair of small paintings, *The White Chemise I* (ca. 1905, p. 73) and *The White Chemise II* (ca. 1905, p. 73) are also very much French in their suggestive spirit. Both depict the same model. In one she looks downward, her thin clothing sliding off her shoulders, and with her right hand pulls part of her chemise to the top of her thigh. In the other, she looks at the viewer, though still in a state of dishabille.

As he had learned from Henri, Guy's execution is rapid in recording the general details of pose and lighting. These early oils and drawings reveal an artist of considerable talent, clearly influenced by his teacher but moving in an independent direction. They also chart out the themes he continued to explore in his mature work.

14

10

11

FIG. 10: **A Night at the Opera**, ca. 1905, oil on canvas, 24 x 31 inches
Unsigned

Archive photograph courtesy of Berry-Hill Galleries, New York

FIG. 11: **Untitled (Woman Curled Up in Bed)**, ca. 1905, pencil on paper, 9 x 13 inches
Unsigned

Private collection

Real life intrigued Pène du Bois more than the stuff of novels and studio models, and he was rarely without his sketchbook. He became a regular at the Café du Dôme and the Closerie des Lilas, finding them ideal places to study people without attracting attention. His days were not all work, however. He socialized with new friends, and even, after a particularly long evening of drinking, taught them to sing "John Brown's Body."

The quick sketches he made outside his studio served as the basis for a series of small paintings. One from 1905–6 depicts a group seated around a table at Café d'Harcourt (p. 67) — a place, according to Marsden Hartley, "where the absinthe flowed so continuously, and from which some very exquisite poetry has emanated for all time."[14] A similar visual flavor is captured in *At the Table* (1905, p. 71). Moody and dark, two men and two women are seated together. Most have their backs to the viewer, and the artist was clearly more interested in the atmosphere of the café than in rendering individual likenesses. Not all of the activities he recorded depicted adult entertainments, however. In *Circus Tent* (ca. 1906, p. 77) his quick strokes deftly capture a group of children enjoying the performance. Another outdoor amusement he witnessed is rendered in *Wrestlers at Neuilly* (1905, fig. 12), a work he showed at the Pennsylvania Academy of the Fine Arts late in 1905.

The spirit of Toulouse-Lautrec informs the poster-like graphic composition and stylish setting of *Couple in Café* (ca. 1905–6, fig. 13), in which the artist conveys the chic fashionability of the demimondaine. *A Night at the Opera* (ca. 1905, fig. 10), with its illuminated singer

FIG. 12: **Wrestlers at Neuilly**, 1905, oil on academy board, 12¾ x 9 inches

Private collection

FIG. 13: **Couple in Café**, ca. 1905–6, watercolor, ink, and graphite on paper, 11 x 17½ inches
Signed at lower left: Guy Pène du Bois

Private collection

15

12

13

standing above the orchestra pit, evokes the spirit of Degas. The stage lights envelop the solo performer in an eerie glow, while the musicians and audience are barely visible.

Fresh from his studies in New York, Guy enthusiastically shared his new European experiences with Robert Henri, who himself had been a student in Paris nearly two decades earlier. On stationery from the American Art Association of Paris in late November 1905 the young artist wrote:

> I have been doing nothing but compositions, and have gotten some very good ones I think. [Patrick Henry] Bruce has done some great portraits. One of a man is particularly good. I saw a man copying your picture in the Luxembourg the other day.[15]

A few months later, he again wrote to Henri, regarding an exhibition in which one of his pictures was being shown:

> Thank you very much for the plan, it's great. What a lot of trouble it must have given you. It was very interesting, and made me know exactly the placing of my picture. I have shown it to Bruce. I'm glad you like Bruce's picture. I think it's great. I am very sorry I can't see old [Julius] Golz's thing. I'm getting very sick of this quarter it's too damned respectable and outside of a few Frenchmen that I know, no one [knows] anything at all about art. The Americans are all as conventional as possible. Some of them actually are in art for the money only. It is a surprise to me as they are very young men.[16]

Pène du Bois enjoyed meeting new people in Europe but he was always glad to encounter friends from the Henri class. These he did not regard as conventional at all. One he saw regularly was Patrick Henry Bruce, who had recently married fellow student Helen Kibbey. Many Americans gathered at Bruce's studio and Guy was stimulated by his visits there: "Here art was talked of seriously, frowningly, with no funny business."[17]

Guy might have remained longer in France had his father not become seriously ill in May 1906. They sailed for home in July — a series of quick sketches survives from the journey — but his father died before they reached New York. Although his father had been in poor health for some time, it was nonetheless a shock for Guy. Conscious of his familial and cultural heritage, Henri had requested before his death that Guy begin using his full name professionally. Accordingly, by the end of the year "Guy Pène du Bois" replaces "Guy du Bois" as his regular signature on his paintings.[18]

16

14

15

FIG. 14: **A Fashion in Stripes**, ca. 1910, charcoal and watercolor on cardboard, 14¼ x 11½ inches (sight)
Unsigned

Whitney Museum of American Art, New York

FIG. 15: **The Law**, ca. 1915, crayon on cardboard, 15⅞ x 12¾ inches (sight)
Unsigned
Inscribed lower center: The State
    [crossed out several times] Law
Bottom edge center left:
    Jefferson Market Court

Whitney Museum of American Art, New York

16

17

Back in New York: Early Paintings and Drawings | With the death

of his father, Pène du Bois was faced with the necessity of earning a living. His father's profession made writing a logical choice and he was hired as a general reporter by the *New York American*, the paper that had employed Henri. While his new position had nothing to do with the visual arts, it turned out to be excellent for honing Guy's observational skills and connecting him with subject matter that keenly interested him. The job brought him in contact with a wide range of individuals and professions, and the experience proved fruitful. He continued to explore the themes he had embarked on in France but now broadened them to include lawyers, actors, politicians, and visitors to art galleries.

Covering the police beat took him to some of the seamier parts of town, including the notorious Mulberry Street and the Tenderloin neighborhood, located not far from the theater district and an area rich in subjects of interest — an ever-changing cast of characters. Places like the Jefferson Market Police Court, located at 10th Street and 6th Avenue, fascinated him and he made images of the scenes he regularly saw there, as in *The Tenderloin* (1906, fig. 18). He studied the prostitutes who had been arrested, recalling: "I also recorded the Tenderloin girls in large plumed hats and bedraggled fineries standing limply if defiantly before the police lieutenant's bar. These pictures, with a few exceptions, were rarely, if ever shown. They gave my mother many unhappy moments."[19]

Pène du Bois was not a very effective reporter, but the scenes and people he witnessed — a mix of prostitutes, lawyers, and bondsmen — comprised a rich trove of visual material on which he drew during the next decade and a half. Like Daumier, he often depicted lawyers

FIG. 16: **After the Music Lesson**, ca. 1907, oil on board, 12½ x 9½ inches

Private collection

FIG. 17: **Opera**, 1907, crayon and graphite on paper, 14⅞ x 12⅜ inches (sight) Unsigned Inscribed at lower left: [arrow pointing towards figure to the left edge of drawing] / Henderson / Music Critic / Sun Lower center left: [arrow pointing towards left center figure] / Krehbiel / Music Critic / Trib Lower center right: "Opera" / date 1907

Whitney Museum of American Art, New York, Gift of Gertrude Vanderbilt Whitney 31.532

who, even in sketches, are identifiable by their round shapes and pompous body language, and he regarded their courtroom performances as comparable to those given by actors on a stage. Typical is *The Law* (ca. 1915, fig. 15), in which his drawing is more broadly composed and more heavily outlined. The ability to capture the essence of what he saw was something he had learned from Henri. The balloon head atop a portly body was long one of his trademarks.

Guy used some of his sketches for paintings. One of his strongest is *The Lawyers* (1919, p. 92), the striking blue background of which highlights the profiles of the two suited figures standing behind the courtroom balustrade. In *The Corridor* (1914, p. 84), three jurists consult, presumably about the case of the woman who stands patiently to the left.

A shift in reporting duties from the police beat to music finally brought Guy's writing into the realm of the arts; however, perhaps because he used the time for doing sketches like *Opera* (1907, fig. 17) rather than focusing on the musical performances, he showed little talent as a music critic. His early New York work is typically broadly brushed, dark in coloring, and small in size so as to be able to be finished quickly during the small increments of time available to him. Other works have music as their central theme, as in *The Pianist* (1912–14, p. 78). Some of the interactions he portrayed are intentionally vague in their specific reference. In *After the Music Lesson* (ca. 1907, fig. 16), for example, it is not clear whether the encounter pictured was from life or was from a stage scene. Many oils depict fashionable people engaged in metropolitan pleasures, as in *On the Town* (ca. 1906–8, p. 74). The jaunty camaraderie of men in formal dress after having indulged in considerable imbibing must have been a familiar sight to the artist, who himself was aspiring to sophistication, wishing to be "a man of the world" not just a "man about town."[20] He was drawn to the bon vivants he saw in full evening dress and, appropriately, his first sale through Macbeth was of just such a scene.

Guy, so deft at conveying human encounters, produced many drawings during this period in which the communication gap between men and women is readily apparent, as are divergences in class and types. In *A Fashion in Stripes* (ca. 1910, fig. 14), a chic young woman in a striking dress and a hat ornamented with a long feather contemplates an older man. The cane to the right on which he leans provides a visual counterpoint to her umbrella at the left. Guy's interest in fashion was reinforced by his marriage to Florence ("Floy") Sherman Duncan in 1911, a relationship that brought personal stability but also family responsibilities. A former concert

18

FIG. 18: **The Tenderloin**, 1906, watercolor and ink on paper, 7¾ x 5¾ inches
Signed at lower right: Guy Pène du Bois

Bernard Goldberg Fine Arts, LLC, New York

FIG. 19: **Shops**, 1922, oil on panel, 25 x 20 inches

Los Angeles County Museum of Art, Los Angeles County Fund, 25.7.3; Archive photograph courtesy of Peter A. Juley and Son Collection, Smithsonian American Art Museum, Washington, D.C.

18

pianist,[21] Floy had three children (Virginia, Donald, and Robert) from a previous marriage and two with Guy: Yvonne in 1913 and William in 1916. Until they went to France, Floy helped support the family as a designer of children's clothes, generating more income than her artist husband.

The tent that serves as the backdrop in *A Fashion in Stripes* is later echoed in *Shops* (1922, fig. 19), another of Guy's early paintings. In this canvas two women wearing dresses with pert white collars and jaunty hats stand next to an iron fence in front of a pair of shops. One of the shops has "Guy Pène du Bois Painter" in block letters above the awning and advertises "Paintings, Watercolors, Manuscripts"; the adjacent one says "Floy Pène" and advertises "Designs for Children." The figures are nearly identical, though the dress of the one on the left is red with a black belt and hat, and that of the one on the right is all black with a contrasting red hat. The stripes of the awning and the pavement are also red. One woman faces the viewer, the other is turned away and bends to adjust her stockings.

20

Guy took a studio on West 23rd Street and painted when he had time. He tried to keep up with some of his former Henri classmates, who also held odd jobs, and participated in exhibitions when he had completed works. The difficulty of being pulled in two directions was eased somewhat when, in 1908, he was finally able to write art criticism. The following year he was promoted to full-time art critic, and he remained with the *New York American* until 1912. Although writing continued to take up much of his time, at least he was writing of the field and those in it. His essays began to appear regularly in *Arts and Decoration* in 1911; the magazine made him editor in 1913, and he remained there until 1915. For a year, between 1913 and 1914, he was also Royal Cortissoz's assistant at the *New York Tribune*. Moving on to the *New York Post* in 1916, he was on staff for two years. He returned to *Arts and Decoration* as editor in 1917. For much of his career, art criticism was a steady source of income and he often wrote for several publications at the same time.

He left *Arts and Decoration* in 1921 and for the next year he wrote regularly for *International Studio*. During the twenties he also contributed to *The Arts*. Although writing took time away from his studio, his paintings did not yet provide enough income to support him. His success as a critic did little to allay his frustration at having so little time to paint, and he declared: "I'm sick of writing."[22] Nevertheless, his period of greatest activity as a critic spanned an era of great change in American art, and he left an extensive body of criticism. There was no more articulate defender of the modern realist tradition; and that he was also a practicing artist gave special strength to his views.

19

21 22

Teaching was another common source of income for artists, and throughout the twenties Guy offered private lessons in his studio as well as classes at the Art Students League. His students included Jack Tworkov, Alexander Calder, Raphael Soyer, and Isabel Bishop, the latter of whom he painted a thoughtful portrait (1924, National Portrait Gallery).

His work as an art critic gave Guy Pène du Bois ample opportunity to study gallery and museum habitués (who, he discovered, had as many pretensions and foibles as any he had seen in professions) and his images of them are unusually pointed. Typical is *Chanticleer* (1922, San Diego Museum of Art), which features a mustached man — in top hat, tails, and spats and carrying a walking stick — striding out of a gallery whose walls have been painted a brilliant red. A portly man, likely the dealer, stands respectfully yet watchfully against the wall. Another rendition with a similar edge is *The Art Lovers* (1922, p. 99), which shows two men in evening attire conversing in front of a painting. The bright red carpet provides a startling contrast to the dark, formal clothes worn by the two men. There is a portrait hanging in the background but the businessmen are oblivious to the art around them. A woman walks toward another room in the gallery, further reinforcing the masculine nature of the presumably financial content of their conversation. The more portly figure at left appears older but their professions are probably similar. Their clothing is an emblem of their social status, and Pène du Bois was amused that they depended on something so superficial to publicly assert their roles:

> They are ludicrous only in the badges they wear, badges that are tokens of devotion to one ideal or another. Badges or marks left by the chains of their slavery. Funny slaves, proud of their chains, strutting in them, and nice in the ingenious generosity of all naiveté.[23]

FIG. 21: **Interior**, 1912, oil on canvas, 15½ x 11½ inches

Unlocated; Archive photograph courtesy of Peter A. Juley and Son Collection, Smithsonian American Art Museum, Washington, D.C.

FIG. 22: **The Little Redon**, 1925, oil on canvas, 20 x 15 inches

Unlocated; Archive photograph courtesy of Peter A. Juley and Son Collection, Smithsonian American Art Museum, Washington, D.C.

20

23

24

Guy's social satire was in the tradition of Daumier and others, but he strove to imbue his works with more meaning. He believed their social content raised his canvases above mere satire: "There must be numberless reasons why satirists are rarely put in the first rank of pictorial art....Criticism, we are constantly told, if there must be criticism, is valueless except when it is constructive."[24]

In addition to writing, Guy involved himself in other endeavors within the art world. In 1912 he joined the Association of American Painters and Sculptors, which in 1913 put together the famous Armory Show. His most important contribution to the enterprise was handling publicity for the exhibition, including editing a special issue of *Arts and Decoration*. Six of his paintings were shown: *Cascade, Bois de Boulogne* (1905, fig. 20), *Interior* (1912, fig. 21), *The Politician* (ca. 1912, fig. 30), *Virginia* (ca. 1912, unlocated), *"Waiter!"* (1912, fig. 23), and *Twentieth-Century Youth* (1913, fig. 24). All styles were presented, but the press—much to the dismay of some of the realists, including Henri, who showed five works—focused mostly on the moderns. We can be sure Guy shared the show's spirit of independence in challenging the conservative art establishment (represented by, among other organizations, the National Academy of Design), for it affirmed his faith in the "youth, energy, [and] ambition"[25] of the new generation of progressive American artists, of which he considered himself a part. Unfortunately, this enthusiasm vanished after the exhibition closed. Perceived administrative irregularities led Guy and a group of other artists to resign from the Association, frustrated at the outcome of what they believed had been a group effort that was eclipsed by the modernists. While a broad range of styles had been represented in the show, including work by nineteeth-century European masters, the avant-garde had clearly supplanted The Eight.

FIG. 23: **"Waiter!"**, 1912, oil on board, 16 x 12 inches

Unlocated; Archive photograph courtesy of Peter A. Juley and Son Collection, Smithsonian American Art Museum, Washington, D.C.

FIG. 24: **Twentieth-Century Youth**, 1913, oil on panel, 18 x 14 inches

Unlocated; Archive photograph courtesy of Peter A. Juley and Son Collection, Smithsonian American Art Museum, Washington, D.C.

21

25

26

Despite his disappointment with events connected with the Armory Show, Guy's reputation as a painter grew steadily through exhibitions and sales. By 1913, Kraushaar Galleries was including his work in group shows, beginning a professional relationship that would last for more than thirty years (the gallery mounted his first commercial solo show in 1922). Not only did they sell his works, they occasionally hired him to write introductions to their catalogues, even though Guy held most dealers in low regard, feeling they cared little about art and artists. His caricatures show them as types — rounded in form and predatory in expression as they awaited customers in their red velvet lairs — as can be seen in *The Little Redon* (1925, fig. 22). But he admired several staunch supporters of contemporary American art, including John Francis Kraushaar and William Macbeth.

Perhaps hopeful he would be able to show regularly at Kraushaar, Guy resolved to cut expenses. Reasoning that if he did not have to write so much he would be able to paint more, he decided to escape the expense and distractions of the city and in 1914 moved his family from Staten Island to Nutley, New Jersey. He soon discovered, however, that those distractions had brought with them valuable professional contacts that could advance his career. He decided Nutley was too isolated from the art world, the main source of his income, and moved back to Manhattan in 1917.

Guy's characteristic themes were fully established by the mid-teens. He continued to explore subjects drawn from everyday life, producing small oils on canvas and panels. In these darkly colored and carefully observed scenes, which had become his trademark, humor is evident. *The Intellectuals* (ca. 1912–14, p. 79) portrays his favorite social type. His disdain for

22

FIG. 25: **"Can You Act?"**, 1914, crayon and graphite on paper, 23 x 14½ inches (sheet)
Unsigned
Inscribed in pencil:
Upper center: Arming the Movers in the Movies
Lower center: Director – Can you act? / Applicant – Sure – I jumped from High Bridge once.
Bottom center edge: Guido

Whitney Museum of American Art, New York; Gift of Gertrude Vanderbilt Whitney 31.525

FIG. 26: **"Come and Meet My Brother"**, 1914, crayon and ink on cardboard, 13⅞ x 12 inches (sight)
Signed and dated at lower left: Guy Pène du Bois 1914
Inscribed bottom center: The fat one: "Come and meet my brother."

Whitney Museum of American Art, New York

the complacency and pretensions of the bourgeoisie is evident in *Mother's Darling* (1913, p. 83), though he tempers his contempt by focusing on the amusing aspects of an aging child with his aging parent, both in jaunty hats:

> Malice is the cartoonist's bête noir. He should avoid it as the canoeist avoids rocks: it is as destructive to the value of his cartoon's argument as bitumen to the lasting value of a painting. He should never descend to gossip[ ] regarding the physical deformities of the person or persons in question. Caricatures should be general and just, and should not delve into the intimate weaknesses which, while they may be seen and may be true, are apart or irrelevant to the reason of the judgement. Only the big, salient, forcible facts are, justly, to be ridiculed by the cartoonist's pencil....For he has to do with actions, morals, manners, voluntary discrepancies, not those that come unsought and undeserved. He must have the force that simplicity lends and, to better imprint his thesis on the public mind, humor, for the world laughs most readily and most destructively. Either of these, however, will rebound upon himself if inspired, enfin, by malice.[26]

During this period Guy preferred to work in smaller scale, believing it conveyed his views with greater strength:

> I cannot see any valid excuse for covering a large canvas with a picture that could be concentrated in a small one. In exhibitions, in large exhibitions where you compete with hundreds of other men it is well to make enough noise, for noise and size are synonymous, to be heard with the rest. It is not wise to be heard above the others unless your sound excels theirs in quality which is not likely. It is in the small pictures more often, when the small picture is considered seriously and not as a sketch, that concentrated and compact energy of expression is to be found.[27]

Restaurants, which provided a convenient place for couples to meet, had been popular subjects for members of The Eight, who often depicted the establishments they frequented. Pène du Bois too favored this subject. *Couple at Maxim's* (ca. 1914–15, Joslyn Art Museum) depicts a New York restaurant founded in 1909; described as a "lobster palace,"[28] it was located at 110 West 38th Street, between 6th Avenue and Broadway. Of his more informal *Hallway, Italian Restaurant* (1922, National Gallery of Art), he observed:

FIG. 27: **Eugenics Again!**, 1914,
crayon and graphite on paper
13⅜ x 11⅝ inches (sight)
Signed and dated at lower right:
  Guy Pène du Bois 1914
Titled and inscribed at lower right
  center: Eugenics again! / "But you
  see, hang it all, the family doesn't
  think you're good enough for me"

Whitney Museum of American Art, New York;
Gift of Gertrude Vanderbilt Whitney 31.529

[It] fairly smells of Italian cooking. A man and woman enter silhouetted against pink wall paper; they are sixth rate urbanites preferring a succulent meal enlivened by a florid orchestra — vulgar but harmless seems to be their label.[29]

Only occasionally did he depict members of his expanded family, and some canvases are uncharacteristically personal. *The Seamstress* (1913, p. 82), for example, is an interior scene painted in his house on Staten Island; seated in adjacent rocking chairs are Floy and her daughter Virginia.

The many drawings Guy made during these years reveal the bite of his humor, which was often sharper in graphic form. Some appear to have been executed as illustrations, though the text that inspired them remains unknown and they were not published. Typical is *"Come and Meet My Brother"* (1914, fig. 26), in which a portly gentleman in evening dress urges an introduction on an older and more slender man in spectacles. The unseen relative is probably their sartorial twin, differing only in weight.

Theatrical themes are common in Guy's work, and he drew on the large stock of images he had made during his early years as a critic. In *Eugenics Again!* (1914, fig. 27) a man in evening attire stands with a gowned woman. A figure in the background appears to summon theatergoers back to the performance, although the woman's body language suggests she might not return to her seat. Especially popular during the first third of the twentieth century, eugenics is a pseudo-science whose focus is on the improvement of the human race through the control of hereditary factors, in particular genes and breeding. For a certain sector of American society, class and breeding were synonymous, but it is not at all clear that a match between the older man and the younger woman would result in any genetic gain. The artist's inscription — "But you see, hang it all, the family doesn't think you're good enough for me" — suggests that his relatives do not approve of their potential union of money and beauty.

Another tuxedo-clad theatergoer is the subject of *Study of a Gentleman* (1918, fig. 28); his left pinky extended, he is conscious of his status but uncomfortable in his role. *"Can You Act?"* (1914, fig. 25) presents a backstage encounter between a sprightly young woman in need of a job and an older, slump-shouldered man apparently doing the hiring. *Behind the Scenes* (ca. 1915, p. 86) portrays another backstage tête-à-tête in which a man in top hat and tails whose face is partially hidden in the shadow cast by his hat confronts a doll-like young woman wearing a pink tutu. Guy would return to this theme in *In the Wings* (1921, Allen Art Museum, Oberlin College), in which two rather ominous ballerinas confront a gentleman (in Guy's preliminary sketch, the male was in costume).

24

Not all of Guy's paintings depict figures in such identifiable contexts. In *Two Men* (ca. 1915, p. 89) and *Blonde and Brunette* (1915, p. 87) he presents the paired figures he favored, and *Social Register* (1919, Forbes Magazine Collection) pictures a balding man sitting alone in an easy chair staring at a heating grate.

World events were of little interest to the artist, although there are occasional references to World War I, but the anonymous formality of military uniforms inspired him, as in *Soldiers* (1919, p. 97). The subject of war was unavoidable in New York; as he commented in 1917: "New York is a parade ground — soldiers going to the training camps — foreign commissions visiting us."[30] In the main, however, he was drawn to social uniforms. In *The French Commission* (1917, p. 91), the artist shows more interest in the clothing worn at events than in the events themselves.

29

By the late teens, Guy Pène du Bois was on the verge of achieving his mature style. His work had become more stylized, and he turned increasingly to the fashionable world of urban society for inspiration. His forms became more simplified as he turned his figures into types, using their manners and the interactions of contemporary life to convey social commentary. As he recognized the importance of these themes to his work, the artist's canvases and panels gradually increased in size and his colors became bolder.

Two of Guy's strongest paintings from the late teens — *Intellect and Intuition* (1918, p. 93) and *The Sisters* (1919, p. 94)[31] — show pairs of women. He depicts them with vivid saturated color, abstracting the volumes of his figures into simple shapes and setting their flatly modeled bodies against boldly patterned backgrounds. Separated from their usual "old rounder"[32] companions, there is something ominous, almost predatory about them. The figures are essentially twins, their respective social roles mirror images.

The paired women Guy portrayed in these two paintings show his passion for types rather than individualized personalities, an interest that saw its fullest development in the mannequin women he painted in the twenties. *Young Girl*, a 1921 watercolor (fig. 33), is an absorbing precursor: a girl in a red-striped dress leans against a tall figure behind her whose body is cut off at the shoulders, leaving us to guess his gender from his attire. The man's hands appear to be supporting the girl, whose face and stance are curiously doll-like, and the shadows the two figures cast create an uneasy atmosphere.

While not modernist, Guy's abstraction of the figures reflects the influence of work he had seen in the Armory Show. Clearly "faces and forms"[33] fascinated him, and it was works such as these that garnered the artist his first substantial critical attention.

25

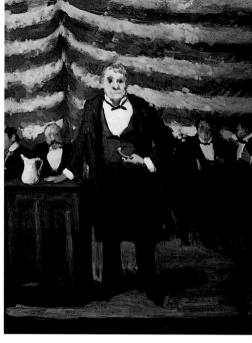

30

31

PATRONS, DEALERS, AND FRIENDS | It was during the mid-teens that Gertrude Vanderbilt Whitney became a significant champion of Pène du Bois's work. She and her assistant, Juliana Force, provided critical support to a wide range of American artists in the form of exhibitions, invitations to social events, money, and patronage. The collaborative spirit of their efforts in many ways echoed the esprit de corps Henri had instilled in his students. Guy took advantage of what Whitney offered artists, including shows and life drawing sessions in which, for a fee of 25 cents, a model would pose.

In 1917 Pène du Bois had his first Whitney Studio show and a year later was given his first solo exhibition there. He became a charter member of the Whitney Studio Club (which replaced the Whitney Studio in 1918) and remained a central member of the group; the Whitney Museum of American Art, which opened in 1931, currently owns the largest public collection of his work. It was the first museum to focus on the work of living American artists, and Guy exemplified the generous support it gave to emerging painters.

26

As a critic, Guy Pène du Bois wrote regularly about collectors and their collections, a topic to which he was well attuned. Not surprisingly, he favored those committed to contemporary American art. His relationship with Whitney and Force had heightened his awareness of the important role played by women collectors, and in 1917 he wrote a series titled "Mistresses of Famous American Collections" for *Arts and Decoration*. Whitney was one of several collectors who specialized in American art during this period; among them were William F. Laporte

34

of Passaic, New Jersey, who purchased several of Guy's paintings, including *Girl with Fan* (1912, p. 81), and Arthur F. Egner of South Orange, New Jersey, who owned *The Lawyers* (1919, p. 92).[34]

As an artist, Guy Pène du Bois depended on the very people he portrayed in gallery settings for patronage, and his paintings began to be purchased by astute collectors with a strong interest in contemporary American art. One of the largest collections of his work — more than twenty paintings — was formed by the wealthy investment banker Chester Dale, who with his wife, Maud Murray Thompson Dale, began to collect the artist's work after World War I. (Maud had studied at the Art Students League.) *Mr. and Mrs. Chester Dale Dining Out* (1924, p. 105) depicts the man whom the artist described as "my best patron."[35] Dale had a good eye and purchased some of the artist's best early work, ranging in date from 1912 to 1928. He continued to acquire works by American artists through the mid-twenties, after which time he began to focus more on French painting. Dale's gifts of Guy's works to public institutions insured that the artist would be well represented in American museums.

Some of the works Dale acquired had amusing titles: *Automobile Tires* (1915, Brooklyn Museum of Art), which pictures a couple parked in their comfortable chairs; and *Mr. and Mrs.* (ca. 1914, Dallas Museum of Art), in which the relationship of the couple dressed in evening clothes is identified only by the picture's title. *The Confidence Man* (1919, p. 95) reveals a surprising ominousness underlying the sexual politics of the chic set, the essence of their relationships starkly set out. Among Guy's strongest paintings are *Restaurant No. 1* (p. 102) and *Restaurant No. 2* (p. 103), both dating from 1924. Set against a deep blue background the evident social discomfort of the figures reveals the difficulty of conforming to the rigidity of social mores. The women generally appear the stronger, with more wiles to survive society's rules, and are shown

27

as a pair, whereas the man is seated alone. Though bored, the women seem capable of action, whereas the man seems devoid of both emotion and energy.

Several of Guy's paintings featured frames by the artist Charles Prendergast (brother of Maurice), who was a renowned frame and furniture maker before he turned to painting. An example of his work is the frame for *Sporting Life* (1915, fig. 29), with its handsome carved and painted floral motif.

The collection of Pennsylvanian Albert Coombs Barnes is famous primarily for its European holdings, but Barnes also acquired many works by American artists. His good friend William Glackens may well have brought Guy's work to his attention. Barnes purchased *The Politician* (ca. 1912, fig. 30) in 1914, the year after it had been shown in the Armory Show. Guy's views of political figures are never positive; William B. McCormick observed that the Barnes painting portrayed "only such a type of man as American politics could produce."[36] It is a view also seen in *The Politicians* (ca. 1912, fig. 31), a work purchased by Chester Dale.

Duncan Phillips and Marjorie Phillips acquired four works by Pène du Bois. *The Arrivals* (ca. 1914) — the earliest work — shows fashionable people enjoying nightlife. The other three works are *Blue Armchair* (1923), *Soldier and Peasant* (1927), and *Two Girls, Montmartre* (1927). Duncan Phillips appreciated Guy's blend of realism and stylization, and praised his "incisive and ironical commentary on life, rather bitter and disillusioned, but very brilliant and sound."[37]

In 1921 Gertrude Vanderbilt Whitney donated *The Doll and the Monster* (1914, p. 85) to the Metropolitan Museum of Art. Her assistant, Juliana Force, the first director of the Whitney Museum of American Art when it opened in 1931, had a flair for entertaining. She liked to dress in the latest style and was known for her striking red hair. She is seen fashionably dressed from the back in *Juliana Force at the Whitney Studio Club* (1921, p. 98).

Jerome Myers, who had been involved with the Armory Show, became a close friend. He acquired two early paintings by Guy — *On the Town* (ca. 1906–8, p. 74) and *Memories* (ca. 1906–8, p. 75), the latter a handsome painting from Guy's early New York years that shows a pensive woman looking up from her papers. Artists often owned work by their friends, but Myers owned few pieces by other artists; that he had these two reflects his enthusiasm for Guy's style.

Others with whom Pène du Bois was acquainted and whom he depicted in either paintings or drawings include Jo Davidson, Max Eastman, Ernest Lawson, Leon Kroll, and Mahonri Young. William Glackens's son Ira studied with him, as did his daughter Lenna, who is the subject of Guy's painting *Art Student* (1934, private collection).

Guy also did a portrait of Robert Winthrop Chanler (1915, p. 88) in which he captured some of the pugnacity of his hard-drinking friend, an artist who was six feet tall and "built

35

FIG. 35: **Portrait of Edward Hopper (Drawing by Du Bois, Monhegan Island)**, 1919–24, Conté crayon on paper, 10⅝ x 16 inches
Signed at lower right: Sketch by Du Bois

Whitney Museum of American Art; Josephine N. Hopper Bequest 70.672b

28

in proportion."[38] As a painter, Chanler is best known for his exotic decorative screens and murals, but he was equally well-known as a flamboyant and extravagant figure with an outsized personality. As Guy noted, "No one needed more space than he and no one could under ordinary conditions feel more cramped."[39] A member of the Astor family, Chanler was famous for his colossal energy and for his parties, at which legendary amounts of alcohol were consumed. Chanler "remained at heart a true bohemian and the stories of his eccentricities are innumerable."[40]

Maine's ruggedly beautiful Monhegan Island had long been popular with artists, and after Robert Henri first summered there in 1903 a number of his students subsequently went there too. During the summer of 1919, for example, C.K. Chatterton, Pène du Bois, and Edward Hopper visited. That it was often chilly there even in summer is confirmed in a period photograph — Guy is wearing a sweater; Hopper seems dressed rather formally for the fishing village. Guy must have enjoyed recapturing something of the artistic camaraderie of his student days. Hopper made a sketch of Guy (fig. 34), who responded with a profile view of Hopper (fig. 35). Hopper's image records his friend alert and engaged in sketching, whereas Guy shows his friend wearing a hat and in profile, similar to the photograph. Another drawing depicts some houses on a rocky spit of land typical of the Maine coast (fig. 32).

During the late teens Guy began summering in Westport, Connecticut, an inexpensive bohemia popular with artists and writers, and in 1920 he moved his family there, although he continued to commute to his New York studio. If he had expected a dullness similar to what he had experienced in Nutley, he soon discovered otherwise. A surprisingly active social life centered around Prohibition-era parties was enlivened by a potent drink made from bootleg gin and orange juice called "The Bronx"; neighbors included writers F. Scott Fitzgerald and Van Wyck Brooks. Westport, it turned out, had as many distractions as the busy city he thought he had escaped and he was not nearly as productive as he had hoped. As he complained, "[M]y old subject matter doesn't come to me here. I can neither write nor paint as I do in town."[41] *The Beach* (1924, University of Nebraska Art Galleries), painted toward the end of his stay, was one of the few major works he completed there.

Also dating from 1924 is *Mother and Son* (p. 101). The deep blue sky and water that form the backdrop for *The Beach* are also striking elements in this painting. The two figures are on the upper level of a ferry; the mother, who is seated, gazes up at her standing son who, hat in hand, appears oblivious to her. Perhaps bored, he is lost in thought.

Guy also painted a portrait of Marion Levy (1924, fig. 36), a notable Westport resident who owned the Compo Inn. She was often late to sittings (to which she brought her friends), so the artist sometimes drank to pass the time, causing him to lazily observe: "The two have made me feel rather careless of my business here."[42] Posed in ermine cape, silver dress, pearl

29

necklace, and lots of diamonds, Levy asserted, "As I stand here, I represent over fifty grand."[43] After it was shown, the painting soon became known as *The Bootlegger's Wife*. Despite the delays Levy caused, Guy enjoyed working on this commission because he found her a refreshingly frank individual: "It is a splendid coincidence when one realist is permitted to do a portrait of another realist."[44]

Despite being relatively unproductive in Westport, Guy was actually at a critical point in his development. During the first decade and a half of his career, his work remained strongly in the mode of The Eight, but now he began to show more of what became his signature style. His technique became broader and more stylized, his palette lighter, his paintings larger, and his vision more distinctly individual. Pulled in several, often conflicting, career directions — painting, writing, and teaching — by the early 1920s he knew he would have to find a way to be able to devote himself full-time to his work if he were ever to make his mark as an artist.

36

FIG. 36: **Portrait of Marion Levy**, 1924
Painting destroyed by fire

Archive photograph courtesy of Peter A. Juley and Son Collection, Smithsonian American Art Museum, Washington, D.C.

SOJOURN IN FRANCE | Guy Pène du Bois turned forty years old in 1924, a year that marked a real turning point in his career. He had finally achieved his mature style and produced a series of important and strongly painted canvases, including *Restaurant No. 1* and *Restaurant No. 2* and *Mr. and Mrs. Chester Dale Dining Out*. The desire to paint was strong, and with steady sales at Kraushaar, the artist decided to give up teaching and writing and move to France. As he prepared to go abroad, he felt poised to take full advantage of the uninterrupted time to work that his trip would provide him, without the wearying distractions of criticism or teaching.

With funds from the sale of their Westport house and advances for commissions from Chester Dale and Duncan Phillips, Guy and his wife hoped to be able to remain abroad for a year (as it turned out, they managed to stay six). The healthy art market he hoped would continue to support him is exemplified in *Bull Market Promenade* (1928, p. 112), in which a prosperous businessman strides along, exuding economic confidence.

Guy was delighted to be back in France — his first visit in almost twenty years. However, even though Guy and Kraushaar had worked out a budget before he left, from the start the artist found it difficult to live within his means. At first they rented a studio in Paris, but the city was not only full of distractions but more expensive than he had anticipated. He soon realized he could stretch his funds much further by moving to the country.

They settled in Garnes, a village in the Chevreuse Valley close enough to Paris to permit regular visits. Guy often took the train in to see friends, who in turn visited him in the country.

His sketchbook was always at hand, and he brought his drawings back to Garnes to make canvases. The Pène du Bois family kept themselves separate from the local populace, whom Guy referred to generically as "peasants." Like many Americans living abroad, his social life was limited to fellow countrymen; he had few French friends and little contact with French painters.

Discovering that it was too cold to remain in Garnes during the winter, the family moved back to Paris for the season. In addition to having to find an apartment was also the need of renting a studio, as it was not convenient to paint at home. Two rents made for additional expense, anxiety over which further delayed his work, creating an unhappy cycle for him of no studio, no paintings, and, without work, no sales. The whole situation depressed him, as he complained to Kraushaar, "I guess that as soon as I get into that studio after this long delay, I'll get over the terrible feeling of despair which hangs over me."[45] France was supposed to be a liberating time for him, but he was often as discouraged there as he had been in America, though for different reasons. At a low moment in late 1926 he wrote to Kraushaar: "Practically nothing else is going well with me. I haven't painted in I don't know when."[46] Realizing he should not make the main source of his support too uneasy, he added reassuringly, "I know that as soon as I get to work again the output should be tremendous."[47]

Attempting to take the edge off his worries by drinking, Guy often joined William Glackens and other friends for an aperitif at a café in Paris. His overall depression, however, made him drink more, and several affairs he pursued in the United States and France had put a strain on his marriage.[48] He recognized that the isolation of Garnes removed him from some temptations: "By seeing nobody I am continuing to keep very sober. Lately I have been drinking a great deal too much. In the last two days I've got almost completely sober — though not cured of the effects of drink."[49] But in truth he did not like to be alone, and eventually even Kraushaar expressed concern that he might be drinking and socializing more than working, but the artist used his low spirits as justification: "Nobody knows how nervous I was during those three miserable months in Paris."[50] He occasionally made an effort to stop, but it seemed to do little for his output. As Glackens reported: "Guy is on the waterwagon and is very much disgusted with his work."[51] Doubts about his painting would trouble him throughout his time abroad. Frustrated with technical difficulties as he tried new themes and worked on a larger scale, yet continuously confronted with the need to produce work to generate sales, he dolefully confided in his diary: "I'm much too slow witted to do rapid work."[52]

Kraushaar had agreed to send the artist a monthly stipend of between $250 and $350, counting on sales from future exhibitions to cover any monies advanced. But Guy's personal expenses were heavier than expected from the start: Paris was expensive and the franc unstable, and the private schools for their children (except Virginia, who did not accompany them) and unforeseen medical bills (Floy had an operation in 1926, and required follow-ups until

1927) added to the burden. Claiming "I have done everything possible to economize,"[53] Guy nevertheless found it difficult to live within his means and remained chronically short of cash. His first letters back to Kraushaar mention his financial stress and soon there was a regular litany of urgent requests: "money imperative desperate,"[54] "broke send money,"[55] "money not arrived desperate,"[56] and "desperate for money."[57] Kraushaar, who must have been annoyed at being regarded as a handy bank, did the best he could but in April 1926 he confessed to the artist: "Business is very poor at the present time due to a big slump in the stock exchange."[58]

Guy assured Kraushaar that he regarded his impecunious state to be temporary:

> I hope you won't think that I have started a long string of hold-ups and that I won't eventually send enough pictures so that you will be able to get back the money I now owe you. Gosh how I wish I never had to bother you at all. But I can paint here, as I'll prove to you.[59]

Kraushaar, patient and businesslike, was firm: "Keep the expenses down as far as possible, as I always want to do what I can for you."[60] The artist, however, believed that most of his problems were beyond his control: "I hope that you believe that I am doing everything in my power to justify your faith in me and in my work. I am living on as little money as possible."[61]

At Garnes he had a good studio space, separate from the house. Once he renovated it and had arranged it to his satisfaction, he declared his ambitions: "I am going to paint masterpieces in that studio."[62] He reported with satisfaction: "I've finally started painting regularly and working harder and with fewer interruptions than in New York."[63] And, indeed, his sojourn in France would be the most productive of his career. Never again would he have so much uninterrupted time to devote solely to his art. No longer was it necessary to squeeze painting into tight writing and teaching schedules: "I do not want to do things rashly anymore. Each thing must be as complete as possible."[64]

Despite his many complaints and delays, the artist made a strong start. One of the first works he completed in France was *Polish Sisters at the Café du Dôme* (1925, unlocated). Not only did he regard it as "one of the best of my small things,"[65] he wrote to Kraushaar that he felt it "the best or one of the best things I've ever done."[66] He quickly finished several more paintings, and continued to work in bursts, steadily producing a body of work. By October 1927 he had sixteen new pictures "of which, I believe, six are finer than any I have ever done."[67] By the following September he had completed another fifteen.

Kraushaar's response was mixed: "The watercolors have been received. Some of them I like very much, and some I do not. So that's that."[68] He did not think the views of Garnes and Deauville would sell well and discouraged Guy's pursuit of landscapes. Guy nevertheless continued to experiment. One of his strongest landscapes was *Valley of the Chevreuse* (1926, unlocated), which won a prize when it was shown at the Art Institute of Chicago in 1930. Rarely would he equal the broad stylization he achieved in that work, reminiscent of the regionalist midwestern landscapes of Grant Wood.

Still life painting was not a genre that particularly interested him, but Guy was capable of producing strong examples, such as *Still Life: Wine and Fruit* (1925, private collection), a work in the tradition of French artist Paul Cézanne. Despite these forays into other genres, however, Guy recognized his own artistic limitations:

> I feel more and more that my pictures must seek interest in the faces and forms of people. I am not a landscape painter....I have never been able to explain my inability to produce good landscapes. It is not entirely a lack of interest in landscape.[69]

During the summer, the artist and his family left the hot city for the seaside. They enjoyed Villerville-sur-Mer, which was cheaper than the more fashionable watering holes but close enough for him to visit them in search of things to paint; at both Deauville and Trouville he found "loads of my kind of subject matter."[70] He busily recorded imagery in his sketchbook: "I'm getting crammed with subject matter here — beaches and tents, casinos and gambling

FIG. 37: **Three Women at Longchamps**, 1927, ink and watercolor on paper, 14¾ x 11¾ inches
Signed and dated at lower right: Guy Pène du Bois 27
Archive photograph courtesy of the Estate of Yvonne Pène du Bois McKenney

with faces leering over green tables, hard-boiled faces, pudgy diamond loaded hands, thin-faced stoics."[71]

Racetracks were ideal places to witness the kind of social interaction that interested Pène du Bois, and his visits to them yielded several works, including *Racetrack, Deauville* (1927, Carnegie Institute, Pittsburgh) and *Three Women at Longchamps* (1927, fig. 37). The trio of sinuous women standing near the fence are all but interchangeable. Two look away from the track, while the third, at left, intently regards the action. Guy was an excellent delineator of the members of the fashionable set who congregated there and he was intrigued by the hollowness of their sophistication. As ever, it was the people, not the horses, that caught his eye.

Similar subjects could be found in the city. *Cirque d'Hiver, Paris* (1926, fig. 1), for example, shows a group of well-dressed circus attendees out for entertainment. Only five figures are sketched in any detail; the rest of the crowd is suggested by outlined forms in the background. The bright red and green of two of the women's hats highlight the overall purple hue, and the fluidity of the watercolor medium perfectly suits the evanescence of their outfits.

Money matters continued to plague the artist. Late in September 1928 they visited friends near Rome, after which, he wrote Kraushaar, "we are going to look around to see whether we could not live more cheaply somewhere in Italy."[72] The dealer's response was cautionary:

> I do not know how Rome would suit you as a place of residence. It is pretty hot in summer, and the question would be whether you would find any subjects there to suit you. Did not know that Paris was getting so expensive. You might find some of the hill towns, like Assisi, Perugia and Siena much cheaper than you would Paris.[73]

By October 1928 they were at Anticoli — "in the Sterne country,"[74] he wrote, referring to the American painter Maurice Sterne, who for several decades had summered there. The visit inspired several canvases:

> I've been painting ever since reaching this place, Anticoli. It is in mountains about two hours from Rome and has been, for years — the stomping ground of Maurice Sterne and Edward Bruce. I've never seen so many beautiful models in one place in my life. If I don't get something out of it I'm a dumbbell.[75]

Kraushaar was particularly pleased with *Studio Window, Anticoli* (1928, Westmoreland County Museum of Art).

Guy determined that the unfavorable exchange rate actually made Italy more expensive than France; in the end, he thought they might be able to endure a winter in Garnes after all:

> This can probably be done by adding weather strips and stoves to the house and settling down to a life of very great boredom and most extraordinary patience. I've started a beard which, though almost all white, will keep my throat warm. However, if you sell enough of those water colors I sent you and could let me have a little of the money we might be able to spend the hardest two months in Paris or go to some cheaper town like Toulon where I would be sure to get fine subject matter — sailors, etc. It is one of the liveliest and most picturesque little towns in all France, and, everyone tells me, about the cheapest.[76]

He ultimately rejected Toulon, realizing he would have a hard time both securing a studio and "finding the kind of professional model of which I now feel very much in need. This kind can only be found in Paris."[77]

Needless to say, his extensive traveling and ambivalence about where to live took time away from his painting. Already aggravated by the artist's near constant pleas for money, Kraushaar was further displeased when he began to receive shipments of work from France.

The dealer wrote firmly to the artist: "You speak of my having faith in you and I have, but when I saw those last pictures my disappointment was great, as the subjects were uninteresting and I do not think they were representative of you."[78] He added, reassuringly, "There is no one who has had more faith in an artist than I have had in you, but I feel that there are certain things that should be looked after."[79] He also reminded the artist: "[Y]our pictures of city life are the best things you do."[80] He urged Guy to stick to the kinds of subjects he did well, and was baffled by Guy's apparent indifference to requests from Chester Dale and Duncan Phillips, who were helping fund his trip to France. Not only had they been steady customers of the gallery, they also had the potential to continue being significant patrons for the artist.

Suggesting that Guy consider reworking several canvases, Kraushaar admonished him: "I hope that the paintings you are sending over will be much better than those you sent before, and I am almost inclined to send these, with the exception of the one sold, back to you as they do not seem to interest people here at all."[81] While Kraushaar did not want to unduly influence his artists, he knew Guy's strengths vis-à-vis the art market and saw that he was clearly foundering in his new environment:

> The subjects that you are doing in the small things now I do not think will appeal to the public here, and some of those who have seen them do not think that the type of work is up to the mark of some of the old things done here. I want you to take this as a friendly criticism as it is to the advantage of us both.[82]

Kraushaar was, above all, a practical man with a business to run: "There is no use in showing the things unless they are top notch."[83] Moreover, people associated Pène du Bois with small pictures; when he began to paint larger ones, sales were slow, especially of the canvases that were too large for easy installation in museums or homes. Kraushaar recognized that the market for his protégé's work needed careful cultivation:

> You know, in your palmiest days you were not one of the best sellers, but I hope that will come in the near future. The public here is still very keen on subject matter, and they have not changed since you left.[84]

Of greater concern, however, was money. Kraushaar wrote in April 1927: "I think you are going a little strong as your expenses seem to be mounting instead of decreasing."[85] Seeing little change, he was forced in October to deliver a sterner message: "I have sent you by cable today $300.00. I cannot understand why you cannot get along on that amount each month, and if you cannot, I think the best plan would be for you to return to New York."[86] He added, with some annoyance, "There is no use cabling me for money, which I cannot send you, as I have heavy enough expenses here."[87] Unfazed, Guy continued his pleading: "My need of money is beyond permitting any sort of ease of mind."[88] By early 1929, Kraushaar was thoroughly exasperated:

> Afraid you are getting in rather too deep for me, and I won't be able to keep the thing up, as I feel that in Paris you can live on the amount of money I am sending you every year....If we are to work together you will have to keep your expenses down to the amount sent you each year and if not, I am afraid we will have to separate....The fact is, I am beginning to think it would be just as cheap for you over in America as it is abroad.[89]

The artist protested in reply: "There's no use saying that I would be better off in America. I've never painted so well as I am painting now."[90] A month later Kraushaar wrote again:

> I am afraid your demands are getting too much for me....If your demands are going to be so high I am afraid we will have to call everything off as I am under a heavy expense here and am doing my best to help you out.[91]

Despite his protests to Kraushaar's suggestion that the artist return to New York, Guy's lack of discipline in the studio was obvious. The diminishment was confirmed by the fact that no sales resulted from the show. Matters were not improved by Henry McBride's negative review in the *New York Sun* of Guy's solo exhibition in February and March 1929. The critic compared his work to that of Leon Kroll, and concluded it was Pène du Bois "who stands most in need of coming home. He has slipped badly this year."[92]

Guy's financial problems, the discouraged tone of his letters, and an increasingly uneasy relationship with a dealer concerned about the quality and quantity of his work were belied by the artist's strong performance in the studio. As he struggled to find his way in a new cultural environment, his work was unarguably uneven, but when he got it right it was stronger than anything he had done previously. Ironically, the artist, accustomed to his days being controlled by writing deadlines and teaching schedules, found it hard to discipline himself when freed of such time constraints.

During his years in France he achieved his mature vision and gained in confidence as an artist. Stylistically, his work became larger in scale, often striking in color, and his figures were solidly modeled and eloquent in gesture. With simplified volumes and tight compositions, he achieved a sophisticated internationalism. Kraushaar was right to worry about the discipline of the chronically insolvent artist, but it was during the twenties that Guy Pène du Bois

36

38

FIG. 38: **Sketch for Woman with Cigarette**, 1929, ink and watercolor on paper mounted on paper, 18¾ x 12⅛ inches 19¾ x 14¼ inches (mount) Signed and dated at lower right: Guy Pène du Bois/1929

Whitney Museum of American Art, New York; Gift of Gertrude Vanderbilt Whitney 31.534a

FIG. 39: **Night Montmartre**, ca. 1928–29 Painting destroyed by fire

Archive photograph courtesy of Peter A. Juley and Son Collection, Smithsonian American Art Museum, Washington, D.C.

achieved the distinctive painting style for which he remains best known and much of his work from this period drew attention.

Both the artist and his dealer were pleased when, late in 1926, Juliana Force bought *Opera Box* (1926, p. 104) on behalf of Gertrude Vanderbilt Whitney, for $2,500. Kraushaar had praised it earlier in the year ("the large one of the figure in the box I think is very fine"[93]) and Guy agreed, calling it "the most important picture I have ever made."[94] Certainly it was a leap in scale from previous work. This painting was one of several he made on this theme. Another was *At the Opera* (ca. 1926, p. 106), in which he presents a powerful female figure, visible only from the waist up, within an ambiguous space.

Opera Goer (p. 107), which also dates from the mid-twenties, takes a close-up view of a woman watching the performance from an upper tier. Her face is in profile and her sleek, dark hair is pulled back far enough to reveal an earring. Absorbed in the action on stage, she seems isolated from the rest of the audience. As in the other two paintings on this theme, the woman has no visible companion, though she is hardly alone, as the orchestra and two balconies appear full.

One of Pène du Bois's strongest canvases is *Carnival* (1927, p. 109 and jacket), first shown at Kraushaar Galleries late in 1927. The night scene was inspired by the Bastille Day celebrations of July 14. His solid modeling strengthened his parodies of the fashionable set. Despite their strong physical presence, the figures retain the anonymity of mannequins in their stylish yet robotic presence. The frozen revelry in which they participate conveys some of the anxiousness of the Jazz Age, emblematic of modern life.

Americans abroad were readily identifiable and Guy recorded them wherever they appeared — at train stations, at cafés, or strolling along the boulevards: "All other national groups tended to merge with the French population, or at least to disappear into it. But not the American."[95] One of his most trenchant portrayals is *Americans in Paris* (1927, p. 111), a work that pictures four similarly dressed women wearing high heels and walking determinedly over a bridge. As one critic observed: "They are crossing a bridge, their handbags clasped as only Americans clasp their wealth, since only Americans thus carry it about, their heads encased in the tightest of head gear and their skin-tight frocks of the shortest, showing an expanse of handsome leg."[96] Another noted that the artist had captured "the hectic spirit of the American woman in Paris, shopping mad."[97] Years later the picture still drew praise. One writer appreciated Pène du Bois's creation of a scene "where four women, cloche-hatted and no-waisted, almost Charleston across a bridge from the Right Bank to the Left.…[O]nly in the music of *Les Six* or in certain Dufy water-colours is that jazzy zeitgeist so immaculately preserved."[98] The interchangeability of his "curious, puppet-like people all doing and thinking the same things"[99] confirms the emptiness of their chic sophistication and the shallowness of their interests.

An especially striking canvas is *Balloon Woman, Forest of Rambouillet* (1928, p. 113), a work Guy regarded as a serious picture:

> [O]ne of these—an outdoor circus thing—is ambitious. I've spent almost all my time on it although it has not yet reached the fluidity I want. I'm working for more color and an easier flow in the lineal composition. Before I get through here I want to do something equal in physical as well as spiritual size to the Massacre de Scio [*sic*] of Delacroix.[100]

His vibrant colors are overlaid on intriguingly static architectonic figures. Several works, such as *Soldiers* (1930, p. 126) and *Soldier and Peasant* (1927, Phillips Collection), treat military themes, and the uniforms indicate roles equally as rigid as those of his society figures.

FIG. 40: **Strollers**, 1930, watercolor and ink on paper, 17 x 12⅛ inches
Signed and dated at lower left:
    Guy Pène du Bois '30

Weatherspoon Art Museum, The University of North Carolina at Greensboro, Museum purchase with funds from the Dillard Paper Company for the Dillard Collection, 1974

FIG. 41: **Sugar Daddy**, 1930, watercolor and ink on paper, 13 x 10 inches
Signed and dated at lower left:
    Guy Pène du Bois '30

Private collection

38

40

41

In 1928 the artist wrote Kraushaar: "I've got two new small pictures, companions, life sized heads of two men in one and of two women in the other which makes me feel that I can still do a satirical thing now and then."[101] Likely they were *Mother and Daughter* (1928, p. 118) and its pendant *Father and Son* (1929, p. 117) in which the children are distinguishable from the adults only by weight. The son and daughter are merely younger versions of their parents, and clearly have already assumed their social roles.

Flappers were one of the central icons of the 1920s. Drinking and smoking in public, they exemplified the "New Woman."[102] Sexually liberated and socially avant-garde, they favored bobbed hair, had slender, boyish figures, and wore short dresses with low pumps that showed their legs and ankles to advantage. But *Woman with Cigarette* (1929, p. 119) depicts an unusual flapper. Neither the androgynous skinny creatures of John Held nor the comfortably sofa-like and matronly shoppers of Kenneth Hayes Miller, she is a hybrid. The scale of the woman, who is heavy and mannish, is disturbing: with caplike hair covering her eye, her cigarette firmly in hand, she has a brooding, somewhat menacing appearance. Here Guy has made a visual analogue of the rich but uneasy characters in the novels of F. Scott Fitzgerald. The preliminary sketch for this picture (1929, fig. 38) shows a flapper more typical in figure and clothing but aging, and certainly no less ominous than the one in the painting.

Paris was hugely popular with expatriate American writers and artists, who congregated in such numbers following World War I that the *Little Review* declared the city the "capital of America."[103] At night, many would congregate in nightclubs and cabarets, such as that seen in *Night Montmartre* (ca. 1928–29, fig. 39), which pictures well-dressed men and women outside "Chypre" (Cyprus). But the true spirit of twenties Paris was to be found in the cafés. The Latin Quarter on the Left Bank was notable for its bohemian character, and its many cafés were favorite subjects for the creative people who frequented them. Montparnasse was the focal point for the expatriate literary and artistic community, and some of its cafés, practically American institutions, served as the headquarters of the Lost Generation. The center of the district was marked by the intersection of two major thoroughfares, the Boulevard Raspail and the Boulevard du Montparnasse. Four of the neighborhood's most famous cafés were less than a block from each other: Le Dôme (opened 1898), Le Rotonde (opened 1911), Le Sélect (opened 1925), and La Coupole (opened 1927). Other places popular with Americans were Le Flore, Les Deux Magots, the Brasserie Lipp, and La Closerie des Lilas (which was modernized during the 1920s). The cafés Guy Pène du Bois painted in the mid-1920s are more modern in atmosphere than the moody fin-de-siècle character of those he had recorded twenty years earlier. The social life within the cafés was highly public. Cafés were places to see and be seen, and several were open all night. There was nothing like it in America.

Le Dôme was one of the oldest. Once patronized by the working-class residents of its neighborhood, it became internationally famous as the symbol of life in Montparnasse after it was renovated in the early 1920s. It was a place where an emancipated and hatless young woman could sit outside on the terrace and smoke a cigarette by herself, a relaxed atmosphere quite in contrast to the formal conventions of earlier restaurants.

Despite the sociability of café society, many of Pène du Bois's paintings portray women alone, without the company of the wealthy men who were their favored companions in his earlier work. *Café du Dôme* (1925–26, p. 108) depicts two predatory and snaky flappers, alert to the possibilities of the evening's entertainment, their jewelry as minimal as their slinky dresses. An atmosphere of psychological tension underlies the apparent smart set.

Café Monnot, Paris (ca. 1928–29, p. 114) focuses on a pensive woman sitting outside a hotel, her back to the other patrons. *Café Breakfast* (1929, p. 116) pictures a typical morning scene after a night's revelry. The seated young woman stretches in the bright morning light, little the worse for wear, and peruses a newspaper while awaiting her breakfast.

One of Pène du Bois's most fascinating paintings was *Bal des Quatre Arts* (1929, p. 115), a work depicting the annual Parisian artists' party. The ball was the culmination of the spring season on the Left Bank and marked the closing of the academies for the summer. It "was an orgy, and no other word describes it."[104] Costumes could be as minimal as desired, and many participants wore little more than red body paint. In masquerade, Guy felt "the opportunity for social satire is limitless," for it permits "almost any sort of comment and no end of symbolism. Costumes, poses, gestures, interlockings. Life can easily be made plain."[105] With exaggerated poses and arresting outfits, Guy creates a decadent atmosphere in the cavernous hall in which the festivities were held. The solidity of his figures and the mysterious space they occupy reveal his painterly and compositional powers.

In the fall of 1929 Guy Pène du Bois and his family moved to southern France, settling in Nice and embarking on what his daughter Yvonne recalled as "the happiest year of our lives."[106] Nice had been popular with artists since World War I, and many came from Montparnasse, re-creating some of the convivial atmosphere they had enjoyed in Paris.[107] Cafés, small in size and cosmopolitan in view, overlooked the beaches.

Guy rented a studio next to that of Eugene Paul Ullman, a Chase student of an earlier generation, and the two enjoyed talking about life and art. Glackens had a studio not far away, in Vence. The stock market crash in October did not immediately affect Guy, although he must have realized that art sales would be severely diminished and that his residence in France

40

42

FIG. 42: **Mr. and Mrs. Middleclass**, 1936, oil on canvas

Unlocated; Archive photograph courtesy of Peter A. Juley and Son Collection, Smithsonian American Art Museum, Washington, D.C.

would soon end. His time on the Riviera was productive, however, and in sketches and canvases he chronicled the sophisticated residents and visitors of the seaside resort.

The most significant canvas from this period is *Grande Bleue, Nice* (1930, p. 121). Mural-like in scale and frieze-like in composition, the painting shows two bathers proceeding toward the viewer as they descend steps to the beach below. The brilliant blue of the sky evokes the region's fine weather, and as there are more extant sketches for this handsome painting than for any other single canvas Guy did, he must have thoroughly enjoyed sitting in the terrace café overlooking the ocean, sketching the changing scene both in pen and ink and in water-color (all p. 120). Some feature the bathers, whereas others capture patrons at tables under awnings either alone, or in a group.

Another strong figural work is *Promenade* (1930, p. 125), which portrays two women strolling along a boulevard, one carrying a parasol should she need to shade herself from the sun. Wearing stylish dresses and hats, they share gossip as they walk. The artist made some changes in gesture and costume from his sketch (p. 124), and tightened the composition to emphasize the upper bodies of the women. *Place Massena, Nice* (1930, p. 123) records a central square in the city. It is a rainy day, judging from the umbrellas, and the woman at right braces herself against the weather. A sketch made closer to the hotel (p. 122) records the many chairs avail-able for those who wished to sit outside in the sun. The warm climate is confirmed by the palm trees, here in the background but more prominent in another sketch (p. 122) depicting a woman sitting at an outside table. In the background are more palm trees and a statue. Although she has no companion, the atmosphere is relaxed, reflecting the artist's pleasure in being in a holiday place, removed from urban worries. (His insouciance would be temporary, however, for in many ways Nice proved to be the eye of the storm.) A small watercolor, *Strollers* (1930, fig. 40), deftly captures a group of fashionable individuals, out to see and be seen, whose outfits convey that they have few economic worries.

In *Sugar Daddy* (1930, fig. 41), an elderly, heavy-set gentleman has taken the arm of an eager blonde with bobbed hair who wears a diaphanous dress. The awkward limpness of the woman's arm indicates both her ambivalence and her economic and social powerlessness. The man, clad in a tuxedo, carries himself stiffly. His expression is dour, reinforced by his narrow mustache and thinning hair. The title makes clear that the sexual and monetary param-eters of their relationship are mutually understood, and the transparency of the watercolor implies the passing nature of such partnerships. It is possible Guy executed this painting before he left France, since his financial difficulties likely would have limited his contact with the American upper classes, at least at first.

In January 1930 Guy received the letter from Kraushaar he must have been dreading for some time: "I am very sorry to have to write to you that the first of April will be the last payment I will be able to make to you, owing to the conditions in business on this side."[108] Guy's daughter recalled the moment: "A cablegram, like an atomic bomb, destroyed everything. The crash!"[109] They returned to America in April 1930.

———

America During the Thirties | Guy Pène du Bois could hardly have arrived in New York at a worse time, and the contrast to the atmosphere of France must have been a bitter one. America was a changed nation, and he did not find it easy to adjust to it. A painting dating from 1936 — *Mr. and Mrs. Middleclass* (fig. 42) — speaks to the lowered expectations of American social life emblematic of the Depression. The sophisticated elegance of Paris is replaced with something more stolid. The couple aspires to the aristocracy but remains class-bound.

Guy resumed writing, but magazine commissions were rare and those he received did not pay well. Although he had been bitter about the bad review critic Henry McBride gave him in 1929, Guy swallowed his pride and contacted McBride in the summer of 1930 regarding writing an article about Edward Hopper for *Creative Art*. He complained that the magazine's standard fee of $50 per article was too low, but by October he had agreed to do it for $35. The article appeared in March 1931.

He continued to make requests for money to Kraushaar, who replied to one he made in 1932: "As I told you when you were here, it is quite out of the question for me to help you at all unless we sell something of yours."[110] In 1933 Guy was so behind in his rent that St. Mark's-in-the-Bouwerie, which owned the building in which he lived, asked each of its artist tenants in similar circumstances to donate three pictures to an exhibition to be sold; Guy sent *Ancient and Modern Styles, At the Piano,* and *Place Massena, Nice.* Two years later, in 1935, Kraushaar's daughter, Antoinette, wrote sharply in response to Guy's admission that he was once again in arrears with his rent: "I trust you will not count on Father for any further help this summer. It is a difficult time for us, and Father has had just about as much worry as he can stand. Of course, if we can make a sale for you, we will be very pleased."[111]

The artist's studio time was limited, and ongoing financial worries made it hard for him to concentrate on his painting. His style began to change again, and throughout the decade of the 1930s his canvases became larger,

43

42

the figural elements stronger, and he experimented with unusual spatial arrangements.
He never completely lost the bite that gave
his best pictures such snap, but it softened
with age as the formal problems of recording
a scene gradually came to interest him more
than social commentary. He pursued many
of his characteristic themes, but his figures
gained in solidity and breadth, and his
Daumier-like humor became more subtle.

Pène du Bois executed a series of
impressive figural paintings during the 1930s,
and one of his strongest canvases is *The
Battery/Seaport* (1936, p. 135). Peter Juley, the city's leading art photographer, recorded the artist
in front of the canvas of which he must have been proud (back cover). Two standing women
dominate the composition, their figures more substantial than his slender café denizens of
the twenties. It is a fine day at the tip of Manhattan. In the original version, an airplane flies
overhead and the Statue of Liberty and a tugboat are visible in New York Harbor.

In *Girls Against the Sky* (1937, p. 137) the artist presents a handsome frieze of three
women, all dressed fashionably and posing self-consciously, as though on stage or modeling for
an advertisement in a chic magazine. Guy's preliminary sketch (p. 136) is lighter in tone and
the composition less connected. In *Hostess* (1935–39, p. 131) he presents an indoor cocktail
party. A woman in the foreground holds a drink in her left hand and turns her body with a bit
of self-conscious melodrama.

As he had before, Guy found public transportation a good place to study people, and
he did several canvases of figures traveling on subways, trains, and ferries. *Waiting/Three Girls
on the Staten Island Ferry* (1939, p. 145) is typical. Three perky young women enjoy cigarettes
and gossip en route. Having spent part of his childhood and the early years of his marriage on
Staten Island, it was a locale he knew well.

Many works from this period reflect the influence of the high color and loose brushwork
of the French Impressionist Renoir, a favorite of his friend Glackens and of whom Guy had
acknowledged in 1914: "Of the Impressionists, the most admired man in modern circles today is
Renoir."[112] Several canvases have a country character despite their urban setting, as in *The Park
(Picnic Staten Island)* (1935, p. 134) and *Along the River/Staten Island Outing* (1939, p. 141).

After Guy returned to America, Kraushaar mounted solo shows of his work in 1932, 1935,
1936, and 1938 to positive reviews. Writing in the *New York Times* in 1936, Edwin Alden Jewell

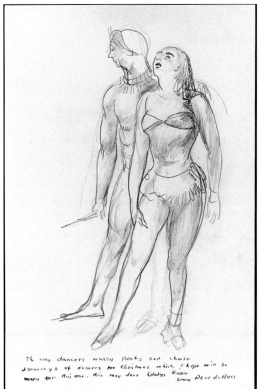

45

43

praised the artist as one of "our most beguiling savants of the brush."[113] Margaret Breuning, reviewing the Whitney's 1940 annual, wrote that the artist "seems completely to have escaped his tendency to wooden figures and strident color."[114]

Despite the economic downturn, Guy exhibited regularly in museum venues and received critical acclaim. His 1926 landscape *Valley of the Chevreuse* won the Norman Wait Harris Prize at the Art Institute of Chicago in 1930; *Carnival Interlude* (1935) won the Second Altman Prize from the National Academy of Design in 1936; and *Meditation* (1936, private collection) was awarded the Corcoran's Clark Prize in 1937. When the artist was made an Associate National Academician in 1937, his old friend Jerome Myers painted the portrait for Guy's diploma submission (fig. 44).

During the 1930s Guy moved past fashionable attire to the social conventions of shopping itself. The artist's *Blue Shoe Shop* (1931, p. 127) gives the figures seated in the background an assembly-line quality, underscoring the sameness of their task. The woman seated in the foreground appears to be exhausted from trying on many pairs of shoes. *Shopper in a Red Hat* (1939, p. 143) is striking in its brilliant colors and strong figures. The woman at center wears a bright red hat with a feather. A ribbon at her neck and her purse are the same color. Wearing a green blouse and a purple skirt, she is framed by a female companion and a young boy.

However well received his work was, Guy could not live on the sales of it. Once again he turned to teaching to supplement his income, doing stints at the Art Students League (1930–31, 1935) and opening a school, named after himself, in 1932. Classes were held in his New York studio in winter and in Connecticut, first in Norfolk and later in Stonington, in the summer. Guy continued to teach on and off until about 1950, when illness and economics forced him to close his school.

The students who took classes from him in New York and Connecticut formed a club they called the Rose Madder Club, named for a color the artist used in many of his paintings. This informal group is celebrated in his painting *Rose Madder Club* (1934, pp. 128–29). An annual dinner was held at the Lafayette Hotel on University Place in New York City, an event recollected by Ira Glackens:

> The gathering was called The Rose Madder Club, but its membership regulations were loose, and it included not only the du Bois students but all the old folks and other

You are cordially invited to join the members of the ROSE MADDER CLASS at dinner on the evening of

at seven o'clock at

R.S.V.P.

46

FIG. 46: **Rose Madder Invitation**, ca. 1934

Private collection

FIG. 47: Sketch for **Jumble Shop Restaurant Mural (Masked Ball)**, 1934, ink and watercolor on canvas mounted on aluminum, 55½ x 40 inches
Unsigned

Private collection

FIG. 48: **Cover of Wine Card, du Bois Room, Jumble Shop**, ca. 1934

Private collection

FIG. 49: **Inside of Wine Card, du Bois Room, Jumble Shop**, ca. 1934

Private collection

44

congenial friends. There were no dues. Reginald Marsh and his wife Felicia Meyer, a du Bois student, Mr. and Mrs. Lincoln Isham and many more were often present.[115]

The conviviality of these gatherings is captured in an invitation he designed (fig. 46) showing men and women in evening attire gathered around a table, clearly enjoying themselves. Cocktail tumblers and wine glasses are prominently featured, and in the center of the table is a large bottle of Rose Madder paint. Humor was paramount. Pène du Bois, "old tomato face" by his own description, recounted:

> [A] line of rose madder and white might help to turn an arm or mold a thigh. But things never go as they expected to. Usually there is more rose madder in the lips and coiffures of students than there is a carload of their paintings. And as the great painter Ernest Lawson will tell you, it is an expensive color.[116]

For two summers (1938, 1939) Guy taught at the Amagansett Art School on Long Island, which had been established by Hilton Leech in 1933. At Amagansett he executed a number of canvases, all infused with summer warmth. The loose brushwork and shimmering bright color of

48

47

49

Long Island Beach (1939, p. 140) convey his enjoyment of the relaxed atmosphere of the seaside. His recollections of *Fog, Amagansett* (1938, Wichita Art Museum, Roland P. Murdock Collection) express some of this contentment:

> It was painted from notes and memory…toward the end of the summer. I had spent most of the summer doing sketches…and was full of information about it. The picture was done very easily and rapidly and is, I think, one of the most fluent ones I have done in recent years.[117]

These are part of a series of cheerful outdoor scenes he painted throughout the thirties, showing men and women enjoying themselves on a warm summer day. Painterly in style, their airy technique and warm tone are imbued with the spirit of the French Impressionists. *Watching the Fleet* (1938, pp. 138–39), also painted on Long Island that summer, portrays another aspect of seaside life, one which intersected with current events. Three women — two standing, one seated — and a man on horseback watch a row of battleships on maneuvers in the distance, a common sight for area residents. Another man, his back to the water, leans against a tree beyond the picket fence and ignores the action. The overall peacefulness of Guy's landscape with its shimmery colors is in sharp contrast to the fact that these waters would assume considerable strategic importance were the United States to enter a war.

MURAL PAINTING DURING THE DEPRESSION | Like many artists during the Depression, Guy Pène du Bois anxiously sought patronage. Commissions and sales were few and far between, so he must have welcomed the opportunity to execute a series of murals for the Jumble Shop in 1934. For this popular Greenwich Village restaurant he took as his theme a masked ball. The array of fashionably dressed individuals and the costume scenes he portrayed were well suited to his compositional skills. The imagery of his canvases echoed the activities that took place in the restaurant. The completed murals were striking. One large panel pictures a large space, possibly a ballroom (fig. 54). A woman in evening dress regards her male companion, whose arm she holds, with curiosity. Dressed in a Renaissance costume, his features resemble those of the artist himself. A trio of figures to the right are clad, as are many of the revelers, in costumes suggesting the late Middle Ages or early Renaissance. In the center, a devilish man drags off an inebriated companion. A second panel features two women and several men in top hats. The distinctive features of the most prominent woman, who wears an evening coat with a fluffy fur collar

52   53

(fig. 55), are those of Yvonne, the artist's daughter. A preliminary sketch shows two women relaxing in the powder room (fig. 47).

The artist also designed a wine card for the restaurant (figs. 48, 49). One could order a Bronx, a Bermuda, a Vogue, or a White Lady, as well as an assortment of fizzes, rickeys, and flips. The nightclub image on the front conveys the raucous nature of the parties held there, with attendees discarding their inhibitions after consuming many drinks. A man plays a stringed instrument in the lower left and a woman lounges in the lap of the porcine man at right. In the background, Cupid floats above the crowd.

Guy had explored some of the themes of the Jumble Shop murals in France four years earlier, in *Bal des Quatre Arts.* A drawing of two dancers (fig. 45), which he inscribed as a Christmas gift to painter Gladys Ficke,[118] is very similar in spirit, as is *Columbine* (fig. 43), an ink and watercolor drawing once owned by artist Gifford Beal, his friend. Guy must have hoped that the success of his murals would lead to further commissions, but none materialized.

The federal government represented additional possibilities for patronage. Franklin Delano Roosevelt, who became president in 1933, worked with Congress over the next several years to enact a series of relief programs known collectively as the New Deal. Several of these programs benefited artists — the Treasury Department Art Project (TRAP), and, under the umbrella of the Works Progress or Projects Administration, known as the WPA, the Public Works of Art Project (PWAP) and the Federal Art Project (FAP).

FIG. 50: Sketch for **Saratoga in the Racing Season**, 1936–37, pen and black ink on paper, 23¼ x 21¼ inches

John Davis Hatch Collection, National Gallery of Art, Washington, D.C.

FIG. 51: Study for **Saratoga in the Racing Season**, 1936, oil on canvas, 22 x 15 inches
Unsigned

The Estate of Yvonne Pène du Bois McKenney and James Graham & Sons, Inc., New York

FIGS. 52–53: **Saratoga in the Racing Season**, 1937, Post Office, Saratoga Springs, New York

Archive photographs courtesy of National Archives and Records Administration, Washington, D.C.

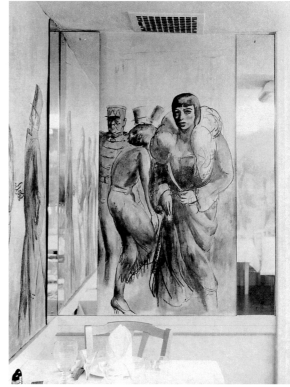

54

55

FIGS. 54–55:
Jumble Shop Restaurant Murals, 1934

TRAP and the WPA sponsored painting and sculpture in federal buildings. Artists, grateful for any commission, were particularly eager to have their work placed in post offices and courthouses, as installation in such prominent public venues could only enhance their careers. But in order to get these commissions, an artist had to be willing to compromise, as doors and signage meant compositions had to be squeezed into less than ideal spaces.

Like many of his contemporaries, Guy Pène du Bois entered several competitions. In 1936 he competed nationally for a series of commissions for murals to be installed in the Justice Department in Washington, D.C. The prominent location meant that winning artists would receive exceptional exposure, and, not surprisingly, a large number of proposals were received. Guy submitted *Emancipation Mural* (fig. 56), a painting that was typical of his best work during this period. Two confident women stride forward in an ambiguous space. The one at left wears a contemporary dress and carries a stack of books in her left arm. The other figure, whose clinging drapery suggests a classical style, points forward to the bright future that awaits modern women. The piece is stylish, handsome, and broad in scale. Although its perceived lack of either didactic content or a theme treating a historical or social issue related to the American judicial system made the work unsuitable, Guy's talent did not go unnoticed.

Because it was too costly to have a competition for every post office, not all government commissions were awarded this way, so work submitted for consideration for large projects could lead to work in smaller locations. Because the selection committee felt Guy's entry showed considerable merit, he was informed that it had been chosen "for special consideration for work under our program."[119] Edward B. Rowan, superintendent of the Treasury's Section of Painting and Sculpture, wrote him:

48

It is impossible to say at this time exactly when such work will be available. However, you will be invited to submit designs for a specific building when such a building, with funds available for decoration, somewhere within a reasonable distance from your residence reaches a sufficient point of completion.[120]

Pène du Bois's name was placed on a waiting list.

Guy's first commission for a federal mural, funded by TRAP, was *Saratoga in the Racing Season*, completed in 1937 for the

56

post office of Saratoga Springs, New York (his first studies are dated 1936). Artists had been encouraged to choose a historical or contemporary local theme, and the fashionably elegant attire typical of those participating in the social season at the track provided Guy with a subject perfectly suited to his talents. One of the two panels he produced (fig. 52) portrays a scene set near the barns and features a horse with jockey astride being led through the paddock area as men and women mill around between races; other horses and riders are visible in the background.

The second panel had to be composed around the doorway to the postmaster's office and needed a creative compositional solution (fig. 53). Guy experimented with several possibilities. He began with quick pen-and-ink sketches that were reworked into more formal studies.[121] His initial conception used one of the local hotels as a backdrop, with a man and a woman standing chatting over the top of the doorway, which supported their drinks as though it were a handy bar (fig. 50).

Perhaps feeling that an obvious reference to drinking in a public building might be controversial, the artist decided to further revise this conception. In his final sketch (fig. 51), for which a study survives, several men sit under a tree reading the latest racing news while other visitors promenade along the street in front of the commodious United States Hotel, one of two luxurious hostelries on the town's main street (the other was the Grand Union Hotel). Homer Saint-Gaudens observed: "Any man who has ever been fond of a horse or caught the flavor of the main street of that racing center will realize with what charm of execution du Bois forwarded his subject in restricted space."[122] It was the perfect mural for the historic town of America's oldest racecourse. The visual possibilities of elegantly costumed racing fans

49

FIG. 57: **John Jay at His Home**, 1937, Post Office, Rye, New York

Archive photograph courtesy of National Archives and Records Administration, Washington, D.C.

FIG. 58: **John Jay Study**, 1938, oil on canvas, 14 x 30 inches

Archive photograph courtesy of the Estate of Yvonne Pène du Bois McKenney

combined with equally well-groomed and expensive horses permitted Guy to explore the kind of upper-class social interaction that so fascinated him.

For logistical and financial reasons, few artists worked in true fresco, and Guy's Saratoga murals were typical in being painted on canvas in his studio. The large murals, measuring 7'4" by 10'5", were brought to Saratoga after completion. Smaller twin panels (5'6" by 3'4") depicting jockeys and the racing crowd, as well as ten even smaller panels for lunettes around the top of the room, were to have been placed above the murals, but these were eliminated, presumably for budgetary reasons. Even in its diminished state, the artist showed his figural and compositional talents to advantage at Saratoga.

As he was finishing in Saratoga, the project he had been promised as a result of the Justice competition finally came through. A mural for the post office of Rye, New York, had been authorized by federal authorities in November 1935, and in December 1936 Guy was invited to submit sketches. Although he was officially awarded the commission in January 1937, his contract was not signed until May. (Postponements due to government bureaucracy and construction delays were all too common for artists anxious for work and a paycheck.)

Guy Pène du Bois hoped he would be able to depict some scene of contemporary social interaction, as he had in Saratoga. Because Rye was located on Long Island Sound, he thought a beach scene might be acceptable, and, as golf and tennis were also popular with residents, he considered those themes as well. But, as he disappointedly reported to Rowan: "Playland and the amusing parts of Rye are out of the decoration as far as the town of Rye is concerned. They hate the beaches. Too bad."[123] He soon realized that he would have to do a historical theme, which did not engage his imagination as much.

Typically, artists would solicit ideas from the postmaster and prominent community members, and as soon as he knew he would be working on the mural, Guy contacted the Rye postmistress, Teresa V. Ball. She, in turn, wrote to U.S. Congresswoman Caroline O'Day, a resident of Rye, for suggestions. Day, a Democrat and a strong supporter of President Roosevelt and his New Deal programs, had been elected to her seat in 1934. She turned out to be not only a former art student but also a great admirer of Guy's work. She suggested that an incident from the life of John Jay (1745–1829), whose family mansion was in Rye, would be a suitable subject. Guy confided to Rowan:

> I don't know much about the old bastard except that he was a friend of Alexander Hamilton and as such not very Democratic. The postmaster herself suggested Jay after having first thought of a great picture of the present cabinet with Roosevelt and Caroline O'Day in the foreground, more than life size if possible. This latter would certainly have pleased the great crowds of Republicans in Westchester. I should think though that John Jay might do. But before getting to work on him, looking him up, etc., I should like to know how you people down there feel about it. I know you are not especially fond of the historical stuff.[124]

Rowan replied diplomatically, "We all feel that the subject of John Jay would serve as splendid material for this mural and I hope that you will be able to work up an interesting design with it."[125]

When the commission became official, Guy still had another month to go on the Saratoga murals. He hastily sent off a sketch with a preliminary idea to Washington:

> I am doing this, although not completely satisfied with it, because you all seemed to be in such a hurry for it. It's too empty now, but with a slightly fuller arrangement would, I think, work very well in the space allotted.[126]

Although the artist found Jay's connection with Rye "a little far fetched,"[127] he recognized how politic it would be to honor a strongly admired local historical celebrity. Jay was

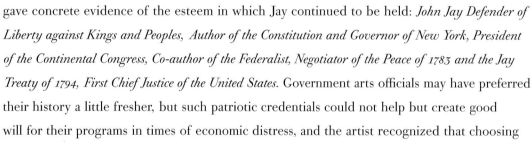

FIG. 59: **The Landing of the Weston Company**, 1942, Post Office, Weymouth Branch, Boston

Archive photograph courtesy of National Archives and Records Administration, Washington, D.C.

59

notable for his lengthy career in public service, particularly as the only Founding Father from New York State and as the first chief justice of the United States Supreme Court. A hagiographic biography by Frank Monaghan had recently been published, in 1935, and its unwieldy title gave concrete evidence of the esteem in which Jay continued to be held: *John Jay Defender of Liberty against Kings and Peoples, Author of the Constitution and Governor of New York, President of the Continental Congress, Co-author of the Federalist, Negotiator of the Peace of 1783 and the Jay Treaty of 1794, First Chief Justice of the United States.* Government arts officials may have preferred their history a little fresher, but such patriotic credentials could not help but create good will for their programs in times of economic distress, and the artist recognized that choosing to represent such a theme made diplomatic sense. That the project had the backing of a powerful Democratic member of Congress was an added bonus. Besides, Guy desperately needed the work.

Peter Jay moved from New York City and settled in Rye in 1746, shortly after the birth of his son John, and built a rambling wooden house to which he added as his family grew. Jay spent his childhood in Rye and is buried in the family plot there, and, although he did not stay in the town for any extended period after his childhood, he regularly visited his father there. After doing some research, Guy decided to present a scene of domesticated history by showing Jay's family and "something of the home and country life for which Rye is famous and also bring in the proud hero of the place, although he was not born there he was, at best, buried there."[128] Ironically, during the 1930s the Jay homestead was occupied by the Rye Country Club, whose activities would have provided Guy with the sort of theme he would have preferred. As the house had been so much altered, the artist based his rendering on an old sketch dating to the time of Jay's occupancy.

52

Pène du Bois sent two proposals to Washington. One was a rough pen-and-ink sketch he included in a letter to Rowan in March 1937, which he later worked up in oil (fig. 58). Jay and his servant are shown on horseback, returning from an extended trip to a circuit of provincial courts within a region extending from Vermont to Virginia: "I have shown them stopping for the night at the Rye house. He must have done this often on his way from one place to another."[129] Guy hoped his spacious view of the home and grounds would convey to viewers that this was a gentleman's country seat. Rowan was not impressed with the sketch, however, and wrote to the artist:

> Frankly the sketch is deplorably empty, as you state in your letter, but our attitude is
> that an artist of your calibre can improve the work with further study and that the result
> will justify the confidence which we place in him.[130]

Rowan urged Guy to supply additional sketches for approval before proceeding to full-size cartoons. Rowan referred to the artist's attractive designs for Saratoga and hoped the Rye mural would eventually be as successful.

Guy's second conception, *John Jay at His Home* (fig. 57), was what was finally approved and executed. Jay is shown standing on the porch of his father's home on the Post Road with his wife, Sarah, and their son and daughter. While Jay's clothing is identifiably of the period, his wife's long dress more closely resembles the evening gowns the artist favored than Federalist finery. Jay's groom stands in front of two horses with his back to the viewer; the horses are saddled and he holds their reins in preparation for departure. The Rye landscape is visible in the background, with Long Island Sound beyond.

Pène du Bois must have been relieved when officials found his new conception "more interesting for a mural decoration" and "a more complete design."[131] Rowan reported that he found the sketch handsome and made only minor suggestions to the artist: "No specific criticism is offered this design except that you might consider moving the main elements, the horses and the figures slightly to the right."[132] (Rowan's close attention to detail was typical of that received by other artists working on murals nationwide. Studies would be scrutinized by both federal officials and prominent local individuals who would often make compositional changes and correct details of historical fact.) In the final version, the Colonial details were made more pronounced: a spotted coach dog stands alert beside the horses and the landscape is more prominent and stylized.

Guy's work on the Rye mural progressed well: "Being the third big panel — with the experience of the others it has gone on much more easily."[133] He completed the 6′ by 14′ mural in December 1937, but installation was delayed until January because of the Christmas rush. The artist was pleased with the final result: "The mural is finished and I'm very proud of it."[134] The postmistress and local residents admired it as well.

Guy received $1,200 for the mural and his contract, typical for the WPA, was paid out in three stages: $400 for preliminary designs in July 1937; $300 when his designs reached fifty percent completion in November 1937; and the final check, for $500, when the postmaster certified that the installation was satisfactory and upon receipt of a photograph of the work. Such an orderly system of payment made sense and put logical controls on the artist, but the government could move with frustrating slowness for an artist in need of money. Pène du Bois wrote Rowan in January 1938: "I want to rush the installation—my God how I need that $500."[135] In March he contacted Rowan again regarding the final $500 due on his contract: "I haven't been paid yet. Could anything at all be done to hurry the check? I need it terribly."[136]

60

FIG. 60: **Breakfast Still Life**, 1942,
oil on canvas, 24¼ x 20 inches
Signed at lower right: Guy Pène du Bois

The John and Mable Ringling Museum of Art,
the State Art Museum of Florida, Sarasota;
Gift of Mr. Harry Spiro

After executing two successful murals in one year, the artist must have anticipated additional post office commissions, but it would be five years before he received another. Completed in 1942, this mural—his last—was for the Weymouth branch of the Boston post office. The commission had originally been given to James Brooks, who was completing his mural *Flight* for the Marine Air Terminal at LaGuardia Airport in New York, but when Brooks joined the Army he had to relinquish the project. In a letter to Rowan in March, Guy expressed his elation: "Your letter which arrived this morning has taken a great load off my mind. I've run out of adjectives—perhaps there isn't a good enough one to use in thanks to you."[137]

New Deal arts programs had long been controversial (and would soon be suspended), and as officials were alert to wartime conditions, Rowan cautioned Pène du Bois:

54

We are not desirous of antagonizing the public in matters of art, and, as you are aware, there are two schools of thought on this subject. There are those who believe that all art should be terminated for the duration and others who are convinced that the arts should be continued as a stimulus to morale and as a growing evidence of the things for which we are now at war. In case there is serious local objection to a decoration at this time I will appreciate your notifying me with the understanding that the work will automatically be terminated for the duration.[138]

Rowan wrote the postmaster in an equally judicious tone:

It has been the constant aim of the Section of Fine Arts, in its work of decorating federal buildings, to integrate the decorations with the locality and to urge the artist to interpret a theme which would appeal to the patrons of the building. We have found

that the suggestions of the Postmasters or local residents, to whom they have directed
the artists, have been very helpful to the artists in insuring subject matter of significance
for the locality.…The artists are particularly urged to use any subject matter in each
locality related to war and defense activities.[139]

Guy briefly considered picturing a dramatic theme of an early massacre of several Indian chiefs,
who, invited by Miles Standish to a meeting, were betrayed by the white settlers and stabbed
to death. The artist decided such an image would be inappropriate during wartime: "I felt that
a mural on that subject would give too much pleasure to the Japs. It was dropped."[140] Rowan
concurred. In the end, Guy chose a conservative theme. If he was disappointed about having a
narrower aesthetic scope, the support and enthusiasm of the local residents made up for it:
"The people are for it. The postmaster is positively radiant with joy," he said, declaring the post
office building itself "a beauty."[141]

Once Guy had chosen its theme, his composition progressed quickly. Titled *The Landing
of the Weston Company* (fig. 59), it celebrated an early historical event. Thomas Weston had
financed the *Mayflower* expedition, but, angered when he was unable to collect on that investment, decided to found a second settlement, at Weymouth. Sponsored by the Thomas Weston
Trading Company, a group of sixty men left England on the ships *Charity* and *Swan* in April 1622
and in August arrived at what is now the Boston area. Smaller than the *Mayflower* but similar
in design, the *Charity* was commanded by Thomas Weston's brother Andrew and the *Swan*
by their brother-in-law, Richard Greene. As portrayed by Guy Pène du Bois, the summer sky
was bright and sunny and the waters of the Wessaguscus bay calm. Members of the crew
rowed the colonists ashore in open boats and unloaded cargo. Visible is John Pedris, one of
the first Africans to arrive in New England.

The local historical society assisted Guy in gathering information, increasing his enthusiasm for the subject he had chosen. He reported to Rowan:

> The outstanding fact to all the people I've seen is that Weymouth, settled a year after
> Plymouth, is the second oldest New England town — a Weymouth man founded Boston,
> another financed the Pilgrims who settled Plymouth. The picture seems to me to be
> in the landing of the original Weymouth group. Sixty men thirty years of age or under
> from two ships — the Charity and the Swan in 1622. The bay is quite good looking.[142]

Guy got right to work, making sketches for a color study now in the collection of the
Smithsonian American Art Museum. His efficiency was in no small part due to his eagerness to
be paid, and he wrote the sort of letter Rowan must have received from many tightly budgeted
artists during this period:

Now, I wonder if there would be any chance of your hurrying that first payment. I really am in very great need of the money. The school is over for the season and its income, small as it was this year, is wiped out. I'd be very grateful for anything you could do.[143]

When he returned his contract a week later he noted, in reference to payment, "I'm praying for speed."[144] A week after that, in early June, he wrote again:

I'm a damned nuisance, but you've got to excuse a man without money. I'm almost half through the final thing, and the first payment's not in yet — no voucher, no nothing. All I've got is an incredulous and somewhat irate landlord. I'm sure it is not your fault — but could you stir the culprit up.[145]

And two weeks later: "I am always crying for help. I hope this does not make you feel too badly toward me."[146] By the time the mural was installed in mid-July, he still had not received the two checks already due him. Not until the end of the month was he finally paid in full for his work.

The Rye and Weymouth compositions were both rather disappointing. The artist was unable to overcome their mundane subjects and therefore did not make the strong showing he had in Saratoga. Aesthetically, the Weymouth mural is his least forceful composition and reflects the intellectual caution of wartime America.

———————————

Portraits | During the twenties, thirties, and forties, many artists displayed a renewed interest in portrait painting and in representing the human figure, and Guy Pène du Bois emerges as a strong portraitist, especially of female sitters he knew well. Although he declared in 1924 that "painting people from memory amuses me more"[147] and, like many artists, he chafed at the restrictions imposed by painting likenesses, he nonetheless could produce memorable renditions when inspired. When he was able to record the features of someone he knew well, or an individual who had a sufficiently strong personality to be able to withstand his sharp scrutiny, he achieved excellent results. His best portraits are of women, in part because their elegant clothes gave full scope to his compositional and color skills. In *Mr. and Mrs. Chester Dale Dining Out* (1924, p. 105), for example, it is the wife's elegant profile and sinuous arms that are the painting's strongest formal elements.

One of Guy's best known portraits is *Jeanne Eagels as Sadie Thompson in "Rain"* (1922, Whitney Museum of American Art), which the artist himself liked so well he reproduced it in color in his autobiography. This large portrait rendered the actress in the role that made her famous, the play based on W. Somerset Maugham's short story. Another provides the features of an actress in *Old Trouper* (1942, Boston Museum of Fine Arts).

Although the identity of *Jane* (ca. 1935, p. 130) is not known, her elegant attire and her strong pose, relaxed yet socially assured, demonstrate the artist's skill with the human form. Several of his other portraits, including *Lisa Mabon in an Italian Costume* (1932, unlocated), a portrait of one of his students, and a related pencil sketch (1934, Baltimore Museum of Art), were widely exhibited. But the occasional student portrait, even of those who were well-to-do, provided little income. Guy most desired to secure commissions like the one he received in 1927 for a portrait of Fern Lombard, the second wife of the wealthy efficiency expert Charles Eugene Bedaux, whom she married in 1917. A native of France, Bedaux had become a natural-ized American citizen and was a millionaire by the time he and his wife moved to New York City. Their château near Tours became internationally famous in 1937 as the site of the wedding of the Duke of Windsor, the former Edward VIII, and Wallace Simpson. Arrested as a traitor in North Africa in 1942, Bedaux committed suicide before he could be brought to trial.

Guy painted Fern's portrait over a six-week period at their villa near Florence and received $2,000 for his work. He hoped to be able to paint a pendant portrait of Charles and was disappointed when the second commission did not materialize. He urged Kraushaar to find other portrait commissions for him.

Several of Guy's best portraits were of those in the arts, and their forceful creative natures clearly appealed to him. Winifred Lansing, a sculptor, executed a bust of Guy while he did her likeness. He painted *Mura Dehn in Dance Costume* (1932, private collection) a year after her divorce from printmaker Adolf Dehn; she had given dance lessons to the artist's daughter, Yvonne.

A trio of superb renditions of his friend Portia Novello Lebrun, one executed in 1939, the other two in 1942, reveal Guy at the height of his talents as a portrait painter. Except for his wife and daughter, no other individual is the subject of so many significant portraits. Details of Portia's biography are sketchy, as is the nature of her relationship with the artist. She was the first wife of painter Rico Lebrun, who had immigrated to the United States from Italy in 1924, but she is absent from most accounts of his life. (Interestingly, although Pène du Bois reproduced the first portrait of Portia Lebrun in his autobiography, only Rico is mentioned in the text.) Rico and Portia were married in 1925, the year Rico moved to New York, where both had successful careers as commercial designers. They lived at 3 Washington Square North, the same building as the du Bois family (Rico studied briefly with Guy). The Lebruns divorced in 1937.

Guy's first portrait of Portia was done in 1939, two years after her divorce (p. 146). The large canvas shows her seated in the studio, her legs crossed at the ankles. She is a tall, handsome woman, fashionably dressed with a strong sense of style; she looks to her left, a bemused expression on her face. When the painting was shown at the Whitney Annual it was praised for its "beautiful fluency of modeling and bodily rhythms" and "refinement of color pattern."[148]

Two other portraits of Portia, both dating from 1942, also show her seated, but at a table. In one she wears a pink blouse and is contemplative, her hand marking her place in a book as though she had been interrupted (p. 147). Her head is in profile, with her hat placed stylishly askew. In the other, she sits with her back to the table and rests her left elbow on an umbrella. Her right arm stretches over the back of a Windsor chair, fingers tense. Her expression is more somber, as is her outfit; the jaunty angle of her signature hat belies her body language. On the table are two wineglasses and a bottle of wine, a pack of cigarettes, and an ashtray. Perhaps it recalls the socializing the artist must have done with his subject. Her restrained demeanor may reflect a change in her personal circumstances, or, perhaps, in their relationship.

Unquestionably, Guy's favorite subject was his daughter, Yvonne, whom he painted from the time she was a baby (the last one he exhibited, *Yvonne in Blue Coat*, is dated 1946). He painted her so often, in fact, that his dealer had a tendency to let people think all Guy's female portraits were of her even when they were not: "[W]henever in doubt about a sitter of one of my father's paintings [Kraushaar] would say 'It was of Yvonne.'"[149] Yvonne was a talented painter herself; she had trained at the Art Students League under, among others, Kenneth Hayes Miller and Thomas Hart Benton. She shared her father's studios and models, and her canvas *Our Studio* (1945, fig. 63) documents their close artistic connection. It was executed at the height of her greatest professional activity, when she was being represented by Kraushaar and participating in group showings at the Pennsylvania Academy of the Fine Arts, the Art Institute of Chicago, and the National Academy of Design. She was not as prolific as she might have been, as her separation and divorce, and her father's increasing need for care during the forties diminished her studio time.

For Guy she was a readily available model; her strong features and distinctive dark bangs were well suited to his figural talents. In *Portrait of Yvonne* (ca. 1935, p. 133) she wears evening clothes and her body language conveys weariness after a night out, or perhaps a bit of exasperation at having to pose yet again.

61

62

FIG. 61: **New Evidence**, 1944,
oil on canvas, 18 x 22 inches
Signed and dated at lower right:
    Guy Pène du Bois / 1944

Private collection

FIG. 62: **At the Bench**, 1947,
oil on masonite, 25½ x 19 inches
Signed at lower left: Guy Pène du Bois

Private collection

LATE WORK | Guy Pène du Bois remained active throughout the 1940s, although he was unable to juggle painting, teaching, and writing as well as before. The beginning of the decade was marked by the publication in 1940 of his autobiography, *Artists Say the Silliest Things*, by the American Artists Group. By its very nature the undertaking permitted him the opportunity to look back on what had already been a long career in art and led to a sustained period of reassessment and reflection.

Heart attacks in 1940 and 1941 were serious setbacks for the artist and had long-term financial reverberations. Guy wrote to Antoinette Kraushaar in January 1941 about all his debts (rent, insurance, food), and by May he was begging her for even fifty dollars on account, reporting in August: "I'm afraid I haven't any sketches here — scarcely ever do any."[150] Floy had a minor stroke in August 1943 and took six months to recover. She had handled all the family's domestic affairs, including Guy's Connecticut summer school, which he could not continue without her help. His health had made it increasingly difficult for him to teach, but after a hiatus between 1936 and 1939, when he was doing his Saratoga and Rye murals, Guy re-established his Connecticut summer school in Stonington. While recovering from his heart attacks, he taught from his bed. Enrollment gradually dwindled, and he found it hard to attract pupils. In New York in January 1941, he was down to two students, and half their fees went to models; in 1943, one student arrived a month late, meaning a delay of fees at a time when every penny counted. Wartime gas shortages that year did not help.

His personal difficulties were exacerbated by world events. The commencement of U.S. involvement in World War II in 1941 further challenged the American art market. The artist made scant reference to contemporary events in his work, although subtle allusions to the conflict appear here and there. The car on blocks in a garage in *That Man!* (1943, fig. 65), for instance, indicates the gasoline shortages common during the war years. Many conservatives blamed President Roosevelt for this, and when the artist exhibited it at Kraushaar in late 1943, he referenced those who would bitterly speak of him only as "that man in the White House." The headline of the *Herald Tribune* in *Breakfast Still Life* (1942, fig. 60) declares "British Chase Rommel." In *Wartime Cocktail* (1945, p. 150), a couple stands at the edge of a room staring in different directions, scarcely acknowledging the other. The general scene is typical for Guy, except that here the man is in uniform.

FIG. 63: YVONNE PÈNE DU BOIS
(American, 1913–1997)
Our Studio, 1945,
oil on canvas, 30 x 25 inches
Signed and dated at lower right:
 Yvonne Pène du Bois / 45

Archive photograph courtesy of the Estate of
Yvonne Pène du Bois McKenney

Guy Pène du Bois hoped to obtain some form of war work from the government, writing early in 1942 to Forbes Watson, who was working with the Treasury Department's War Finance Division organizing exhibitions and posters by combat artists to promote the sale of war bonds: "I want to do something for the government and don't know how to go about it."[151] Guy thought military portraits or didactic murals might be a possibility:

> I could do the portraits and would like to see if, in them, I could not regain some of the majesty which was thrown overboard by the over-soft past decades. I could bring some of that important quality to bear on heroic murals I think. Also I believe I could do pictures of great gatherings of people such as when Churchill addressed the Senate. These things must have historical and propaganda value.[152]

Homer Saint-Gaudens, who was a lieutenant colonel with the Army Corps of Engineers and an assistant in the Operations and Training Branch of the Troops Division, informed Guy in March 1942 that there was no position available in his office, but suggested that he contact the War Department's Bureau of Public Relations within its Pictorial Branch. That office was supervised by Hermann W. Williams, Jr., who had been an assistant curator at the Metropolitan Museum of Art in New York: "The section will have a number of artists, possibly commissioned, who will go into the field with our task forces and move in and about the camps in this land to record army activities. Another group of artists are to paint portraits."[153] But despite Guy's assurances that he was fully recovered from his two heart attacks, the fact that he was fifty-eight years old likely worked against him. In any event, he was not able to secure wartime employment with the government.

During the summer of 1945 Guy had produced only two paintings and alerted Antoinette Kraushaar, who had taken over many of the gallery's day-to-day operations as her father's health deteriorated, that he would not be ready for the November exhibition that had been planned. In 1945 he received word that he had been awarded a $2,400 prize to produce illustrations for *South Wind* by Norman Douglas for the Limited Editions Club, but when the publisher wanted to use them without paying him, he took them back and they were never published.

64

FIG. 64: **Untitled (Two Courtroom Scenes)**, ca. 1945, ink, pencil, and crayon on paper, 11⅞ x 8½ inches Unsigned

The Estate of Yvonne Pène du Bois McKenney and James Graham & Sons, Inc., New York

FIG. 65: **That Man!**, 1943, oil on canvas, 25 x 30 inches Signed and dated at lower right: Guy Pene du Bois '43

Unlocated; Archive photograph courtesy of Peter A. Juley and Son Collection, Smithsonian American Art Museum, Washington, D.C.

In 1946 John Kraushaar died and Antoinette took over the business with her brother Charles (she would assume sole ownership in 1950). The following year Guy and Kraushaar Galleries, which had represented him for more than a quarter century, decided to part ways. Guy had been given solo shows in 1942, 1943, and 1946, but his work had not sold well. The rupture finally came over a disagreement over a commission due the gallery that the artist, as ever in need of funds, had kept. The feelings that precipitated the split had been building for years. Antoinette Kraushaar wrote him in a typically straightforward and business-like manner:

> I realize from your letter that you feel that the Gallery has treated you very badly, and I am sorry about this. I know that you were becoming more and more dissatisfied with our handling of your work, and as I cannot see that there could be anything except increasing bitterness and difficulty in our dealings, I feel sure that neither you nor we would find it of any advantage to continue our present arrangement. We would like to settle this matter before you leave for the Summer, so that the things to be returned could be sent down to your studio immediately.... We have been too deeply interested in your work for many years not to regret this very much, and I hope that you will feel as I do that since it is an arrangement no longer satisfactory to either you or the Gallery, we should conclude in as friendly a manner as possible.[154]

Since he owed Kraushaar money, it was agreed that the artist would leave seven works (six oil paintings and one watercolor) in settlement. The eighty-six paintings remaining in the gallery's inventory would be returned to him.

Although Guy Pène du Bois was bitter about leaving the Kraushaar Galleries, an event which must have represented a serious professional blow to him, in truth it was not the gallery's fault that the art market had changed so dramatically since it had first shown Guy's work, more than thirty years earlier. Overwhelmed by his desperate financial situation, Guy hoped to find another dealer to represent him, but even though the owner of Milch Galleries showed some interest, no gallery could commit to an artist whose work failed to sell. It was not an easy time for an aging artist.

As Guy continued to explore the themes that had always interested him, his style changed once again. His color became more monochromatic, infused with eerie blues and greens, and his brushwork became looser and his figures less solid. Often the wit is there, but the mood is more nostalgic.

From the start of his career the artist had painted from the nude, and his figures grew in solidity. One of his most monumental from his later years is *Peruvian Indian* (1941, p. 149). The model was a woman of Incan descent: "The flesh tones and sturdy build of the girl make an interesting contrast with the spiral folds of her turban and the soft drape of the gown she has just unzipped."[155]

The Puritan (ca. 1945, p. 152) returns to one of Guy's earliest themes — a man and woman in evening dress in an ambiguous space. The woman's back is to the viewer and the round bald head of her companion is made clearly visible by the light hitting it. The man's affluence contrasts with the daunting challenges and sober garb of the nation's first colonists. Guy's mysterious *The Beauty* (ca. 1946, p. 154) was inspired by an actress in the French film *Beauty and the Beast*, who is shown holding a mirror in her left hand and gazing pensively to the left. The painting is similar in tone to *Dramatic Moment* (1946, p. 155), in which a seated woman in a low-cut evening dress apparently awaits a visitor. In *The Ace of Spades* (1945, p. 151) a man and woman are shown reading fortunes at a cardtable; another woman, who stands looking over the man's shoulder, is shocked at the appearance of the "death card." The work was given by the Milch Galleries to the Art Students League in order to settle a $500 advance given when Guy was in the hospital.

Some of Pène du Bois's strongest works from the forties are part of a series of remarkable courtroom scenes. Loose in style and infused with mysterious colors, they continue the exploration of a type he began decades earlier, when he was a police reporter. In *New Evidence* (1944, fig. 61), two lawyers are seated at a table, consulting over the information they have just received. Another man stands to the side. Beyond the balustrade, two standing men in suits discuss the case. One raises his hand to cover his face so others cannot see what he is saying. More loosely brushed is *Addressing the Jury* (1947, p. 156). Jurors listen to the lawyer making his summation, while a man stands before the bench, talking to the judge. It is close in style to Guy's untitled drawing of two courtroom scenes (ca. 1945, fig. 64).

Another painting from the mid-1940s features two figures in a courtroom (p. 153). The lawyer at right, his jacket buttoned and his pose suggesting pleading, attempts to convince the other of something likely related to the sketchy figures in the background. The body language and facial expression of the figure at left, whose jacket is unbuttoned, indicate he is not successful. The artist's late courtroom scenes are generally dominated by the men who were the powerful players of America's legal system. In *At the Bench* (1947, fig. 62), a woman defendant stands with her back to the viewer beside her lawyer who presents a document to the judge. She stands stiffly (and, in her nervousness, oblivious to the fact that her slip is showing), and the questioning expression on her lawyer's face suggests that the outcome is uncertain.

Generally apolitical throughout his career, preferring to portray politicians as a type rather than express any partisan views, Guy's output became increasingly conservative. In 1945 he agreed to be listed as one of fifty-five initiating sponsors for the Independent Citizens' Committee of the Arts, Sciences and Professions. Sculptor Jo Davidson was chairman and a number of visual artists were involved, among them Louis Bouché, Philip Evergood, Leon Kroll, Boardman Robinson, John Sloan, Raphael Soyer, Max Weber, and William Zorach. The committee's purpose, as stated in its bylaws, was "to promote and cultivate the continuance and extension of the democratic way of life in the United States," as well as "to combat all regressive and reactionary forces and tendencies calculated to circumscribe or limit in any way the continuance and extension of the democratic way of life in the United States." Members also hoped to spread democracy abroad and "to promote a speedy and complete victory over the enemies of the United States in the present war."[156] That he had permitted his name to be used in connection with such a cause undoubtedly had to do with the involvement of several old friends, for he seldom allied himself with groups such as this.

Even as his activity in the studio slowed, Guy continued to receive recognition as an artist. *Cocktails* (1945, Metropolitan Museum of Art), which depicts an outdoor party in Stonington, was awarded the First Altman Prize ($1,200) at the National Academy of Design's 120th Annual, although by then the Academy had long ceased to be one of America's most significant art organizations. Once central to the success of an artist's career, the twin onslaughts of The Eight and the American avant-garde had essentially sidelined the venerable institution, and by the time Guy Pène du Bois was made an Associate Academician in 1937 and a full Academician in 1940, the titles were not the honor they once were. Guy found himself, as did many representational artists of his generation, increasingly out of touch with contemporary developments.

When Helen Appleton Read, who also had studied with Henri, organized "Robert Henri and Five of His Pupils," a show for the Century Association, Pène du Bois must have been gratified to have been one of the five included, along with George Bellows, Eugene Speicher, Rockwell Kent, and Edward Hopper. The show took on enhanced meaning in postwar America. As Read observed: "This exhibition comes at an auspicious time. In the social and political world accepted institutions are being tested and examined in order to isolate those which have a permanent and a proven value for the American way of life."[157] While honoring Guy's connection to the teacher who had shaped the course of his career, the 1946 show also reinforced the fact that his work now reflected the past rather than the future. It was a familiar process of becoming part of the establishment — the former progressive, who had been a student of

63

someone himself once a rebel, had become part of the old guard. With Jackson Pollock's first New York exhibit in 1943, Abstract Expressionism had already signaled the eclipse of Pène du Bois's generation of Henri-trained realists.

Despite the family's financial problems, Guy was able to manage an extended visit to New Orleans in the spring of 1946. He and Yvonne took a studio on Dauphine Street in the French Quarter, and from their wrought-iron balcony they could see the famous cathedral on Jackson Square. Guy made sketches of French restaurants and some Mardi Gras group compositions, one of which was titled *New Orleans Mood*, that he intended to work up as finished canvases when he returned to his New York studio. He was pleased when the art department at Louisiana State University in Baton Rouge invited him to give a talk, as he was when he learned that he had been awarded a prize of $1,000 from the Salmagundi Club for *After Dinner Speaker* (though he was frustrated at how long it took for the check to arrive). The summer was spent quietly in Stonington, as he had closed his school. Although he would have welcomed the income students provided, he was relieved not to have to teach.

A crushing blow came in September 1950 with the death of Guy's wife, who had suffered a major stroke in March 1949, the year he was diagnosed with cancer. "She is so much a part of me,"[158] he once wrote, and his was, in the words of Josephine Nivison Hopper, a "great grief... Guy is a lost soul; at least for the time being."[159] Floy's passing concluded a series of devastating personal losses in the forties: Gertrude Vanderbilt Whitney in 1942, John Kraushaar in 1946, and Juliana Force in 1948. (Appropriately, in 1949 he was a contributor to the Whitney Museum's memorial exhibition and catalogue honoring Force.) The string of personal and professional tragedies must have been quite overwhelming, and the many changes made Guy discouraged about his work. His sadness accelerated his steady estrangement from the contemporary art world, which he now acknowledged had passed him by: "My life is considerably changed. Little is left of the old order, customs, way of living. Age is beginning to tell."[160]

Never a modernist, Guy found the works by members of the ascendant New York School as incomprehensible as the criticism published to explain it. He dismissed it all as being merely fashionable, without lasting substance. In the early 1950s, with his old friend Hopper, former students Raphael Soyer and Isabel Bishop, and several others, Guy became involved with a new journal, titled *Reality: A Journal of Artists' Opinions*, which published its first issue in the spring of 1953. Its conservative tone shows just how far out of touch the artist was with current art trends. He and his fellow realists were understandably frustrated, apparently turning a blind eye to the fact that they, too, had usurped an earlier generation. It was hard for Guy to recognize that this was just part of an ongoing process. As a young artist at the beginning of his career he had happily challenged the status quo. His vantage changed when he found himself part of the old guard.

The 1950s were not productive years for him. He painted only sporadically, and did not have the energy to complete a major work. His health continued to decline, and another heart attack in 1953 further eroded his energies. With Floy gone, Yvonne took responsibility for her father.

Another Expulsion (1950, p. 157) signals the artist's estrangement from the art world, though with his typical biting humor. A School of Paris abstract figure in the style of Picasso expels Masaccio's disconsolate figures of Adam and Eve from the Brancacci Chapel in Florence. European modernism had finally displaced those representational styles whose roots go back to the Italian Renaissance. The painting was shown at the National Academy of Design and provides a fitting end to the artist's career.

In the summer of 1953, Guy and Yvonne left for Paris for an indefinite period. His lifelong appreciation of France and French culture remained strong in his old age, and he hoped time there would revive him mentally and artistically. In *Café de Flore* (1954, pp. 158–59), his last dated painting, he returned to the kind of subject he had pursued fifty years earlier as a young art student flush with excitement at his first trip abroad. Recording a landmark café popular with Surrealists, Existentialists, and tourists, his continuing pleasure in the daily life of the French capital is evident. He returned to the United States in 1956 and died two years later, in the summer of 1958, at his daughter's home in Boston. Hopper wrote to Yvonne:

> One can say little that will lessen your and our sorrow over Guy's death, except that
> I think he had a good and full life. He had a brilliant mind and an affectionate nature
> which drew many friends to him. He certainly was the best friend I had in art….Jo
> and I join in our great regret for his passing. He can never be replaced in our interest
> and affection.[161]

Hopper's sorrowful words at the passing of an artist-friendship that had endured since their student days form a fitting epitaph for one of America's most urbane artists.

Café d'Harcourt | ca. 1905–6, oil on canvas board, 12⅞ x 9⅜ inches | signed at lower right: Guy du Bois

Bernard Goldberg Fine Arts, LLC

Untitled (Woman Pulling Up Her Stockings) | 1905, oil on panel, 9⅜ x 12⅝ inches | signed and dated at lower left: G.P.B. '05

Lois Wagner Fine Arts, New York

69

Lady in Bed | 1905, oil on panel, 13 x 9¼ inches | signed and dated at lower right: Guy Pène du Bois 1905

Private collection

Paris Street Scene | ca. 1905, oil on canvas, 31¾ x 25½ inches | unsigned

Kraushaar Galleries, New York

At the Table | 1905, oil on panel, 9⅜ x 12⅞ inches | signed and dated at lower right: G.P.B. 05

Bernard Goldberg Fine Arts, LLC, New York

Untitled (Woman in Parlor) | 1905, oil on panel, 8 x 10 inches | signed at lower left: Guy Pène du Bois

Private collection

71

 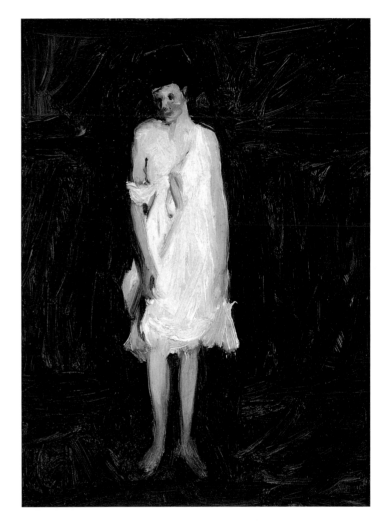

The White Chemise I and **The White Chemise II** | ca. 1905, oil on panel, each 12¼ x 9¼ inches | unsigned

Private collection

On the Town | ca. 1906–8, oil on panel, 12¼ x 9¼ inches | unsigned

Private collection

Memories | ca. 1906–8, oil on panel, 12¼ x 9¼ inches | unsigned

Private collection

Circus Tent | ca. 1906, oil on canvas, 18 x 24 inches | unsigned

Bernard Goldberg Fine Arts, LLC, New York

The Pianist | ca. 1912–14, oil on canvas, 12 x 16 inches | signed verso: Guy Pène du Bois

Private collection

79

The Intellectuals | ca. 1912–14, oil on panel, 20 x 15 inches | signed on verso

Archive photograph courtesy of the Estate of Yvonne Pène du Bois McKenney

Girl with Fan | 1912, oil on canvas, 16¼ x 12¼ inches | signed and dated at lower right: G.P.B. 12

James Graham & Sons, Inc., New York

The Seamstress | 1913, oil on canvas, 24 x 18½ inches | signed and dated at lower right: Guy Pène du Bois 1913

Lehigh University Permanent Collection, Bethlehem, Pennsylvania; Gift of Ralph L. Wilson

83

Mother's Darling | 1913, oil on canvas, 16 x 12 inches | signed and dated at lower right: Guy Pène du Bois '13

Delaware Art Museum, Wilmington; F.V. du Pont Acquisition Fund and Acquisition Fund, 1991; DAM #1991-128

84

The Corridor, 1914, oil on canvas, 28¼ x 21¼ inches | signed and dated at lower right: Guy Pène du Bois / 1914

The Collection of The Newark Museum, New Jersey; Gift of Mrs. Felix Fuld, 1925

The Doll and the Monster | 1914, oil on wood, 20 x 15 inches | signed and dated at lower right: Guy Pène du Bois / 1914

The Metropolitan Museum of Art, New York; Gift of Mrs. Harry Payne Whitney, 1921, 21.47

Behind the Scenes | ca. 1915, oil on panel, 12¼ x 9¼ inches | signed verso: Guy Pène du Bois

Bernard Goldberg Fine Arts, LLC, New York

Blonde and Brunette | 1915, oil on panel, 20 x 15 inches | signed at lower left: Guy Pène du Bois

Whitney Museum of American Art, New York; Gift of Gertrude Vanderbilt Whitney 31.187

Portrait of Robert Winthrop Chanler | 1915, oil on canvas, 20 x 15 inches | unsigned

Whitney Museum of American Art, New York; Gift of Gertrude Vanderbilt Whitney 31.185

89

Two Men | ca. 1915, oil on wood panel, 20 x 15 inches | unsigned

Whitney Museum of American Art, New York; Gift of Gertrude Vanderbilt Whitney 31.186

The French Commission | 1917, oil on panel, 21½ x 16½ inches | signed at lower right: Guy Pène du Bois

Private collection; Archive photograph courtesy of Berry-Hill Galleries, New York

The Lawyers | 1919, oil on wood, 20 x 15⅛ inches | signed and dated lower right: Guy Pène du Bois / 1919

Hirshhorn Museum and Sculpture Garden, Smithsonian Institution, Washington, D.C.; Gift of Joseph H. Hirshhorn, 1966

93

Intellect and Intuition | 1918, oil on panel, 20 x 15 inches | unsigned

Private collection

94

The Sisters | 1919, oil on panel, 20 x 15 inches | signed and dated lower right: Guy Pène du Bois '19

Curtis Galleries, Minneapolis

The Confidence Man | 1919, oil on panel, 20⅛ x 15¼ inches | signed and dated at lower right: Guy Pène du Bois / '19

Brooklyn Museum of Art; Gift of The Chester Dale Estate 63.148.3

Soldiers | 1919, oil on wood panel, 20 x 15 inches | signed at lower left: Guy Pène du Bois '19

Private collection

Juliana Force at the Whitney Studio Club | 1921, oil on wood, 20 x 15 inches | signed center right in oil paint: Guy Pene du Bois 1921 [?] [date not clearly visible]

Whitney Museum of American Art, New York; Gift of Mr. and Mrs. James S. Adams in memory of Philip K. Hutchins 51.43

99

The Art Lovers | 1922, oil on wood panel, 20 x 25 inches | signed and dated at lower left: Guy Pène du Bois '22

Private collection; Archive photograph courtesy of Martha Parrish & James Reinish, Inc., New York

Mother and Son | 1924, oil on panel, 20 x 15 inches | signed and dated lower left: Guy Pène du Bois '24

Michael Owen Collection, New York; Photograph courtesy of Owen Gallery, New York

Restaurant, No. 1 | 1924, oil on panel, 19½ x 14¾ inches | signed and dated at lower right: Guy Pène du Bois '24

The Art Institute of Chicago; Gift of the Chester Dale Collection 1950.1356

Restaurant, No. 2 | 1924, oil on panel, 19½ x 14¾ inches | signed at lower right: Guy Pène du Bois

The Art Institute of Chicago; Gift of the Chester Dale Collection 1950.1357

Opera Box | 1926, oil on canvas, 57½ x 45¼ inches | signed and dated at lower right: Guy Pène du Bois '26

Whitney Museum of American Art, New York; Purchase 31.184

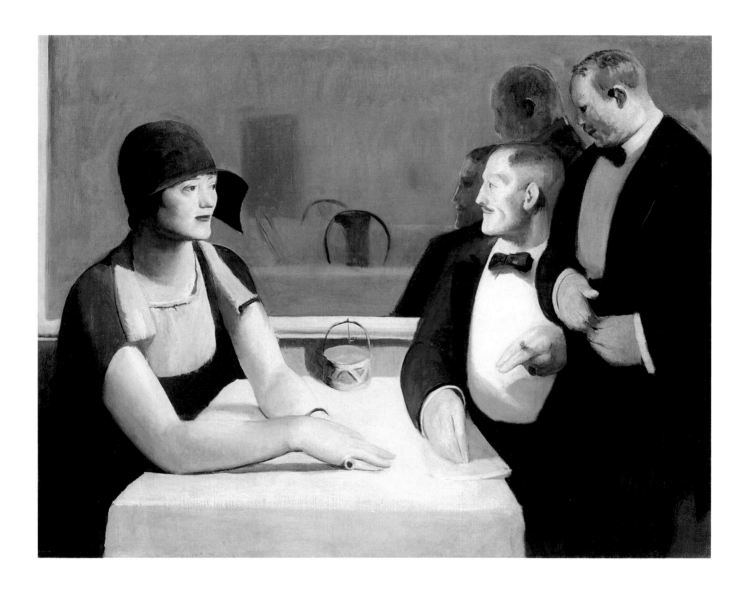

105

Mr. and Mrs. Chester Dale Dining Out | 1924, oil on canvas, 30 x 40 inches | unsigned

The Metropolitan Museum of Art, New York; Gift of Chester Dale, 1963, 63.138.1

106

At the Opera | ca. 1926, oil on canvas, 20 x 24 inches | unsigned

Sordoni Art Gallery, Wilkes University, Wilkes-Barre, Pennsylvania, Permanent Collection, 1997.03

Opera Goer | ca. 1926, oil on canvas, 21¾ x 18 inches | unsigned

Private collection

Café du Dôme | 1925–26, oil on wood, 21¾ x 18¼ inches | signed and dated at lower left: Guy Pène du Bois '25 | signed and dated at lower right: Guy Pène du Bois '26

National Gallery of Art, Chester Dale Collection, Washington, D.C.

Carnival | 1927, oil on canvas, 36¼ x 28¾ inches | unsigned

Private collection

Americans in Paris | 1927, oil on canvas, 28¾ x 36⅜ inches | signed and dated at lower left: Guy Pène du Bois / 27

The Museum of Modern Art, New York; Given anonymously

Bull Market Promenade | 1928, oil on canvas, 18 x 22 inches | signed at lower left: Guy Pène du Bois

Private collection

Balloon Woman, Forest of Rambouillet (Fête Champetre) | 1928, oil on canvas, 36¼ x 29 inches | signed and dated at lower left: Guy Pène du Bois/28

Whitney Museum of American Art, New York; Mrs. Percy Uris Bequest 85.49.3

Café Monnot, Paris | ca. 1928–29, oil on canvas, 22 x 18½ inches | unsigned

Whitney Museum of American Art, New York; Gift of Rita and Daniel Fraad, Jr. 66.124

Bal des Quatre Arts, 1929, oil on canvas, 28¾ x 36 inches | signed and dated at lower left: Guy Pène du Bois '29

The David and Alfred Smart Museum of Art, The University of Chicago; Gift of William Benton

Café Breakfast | 1929, oil on canvas, 36⅛ x 32 inches | signed and dated at lower right: Guy Pène du Bois '29

Archive photograph courtesy of the Estate of Yvonne Pène du Bois McKenney

Father and Son | 1929, oil on canvas, 21½ x 18 inches | signed and dated at lower right: Guy Pène du Bois / 29

Whitney Museum of American Art, New York; Purchase 31.179

Mother and Daughter | 1928, oil on canvas, 21¾ x 18 inches | signed and dated at lower right: Guy Pène du Bois / 28

Whitney Museum of American Art, New York; Purchase 31.183

Woman with Cigarette | 1929, oil on canvas, 36¼ x 28¾ inches | signed and dated at lower left: Guy Pène du Bois 29

Whitney Museum of American Art, New York; Gift of Gertrude Vanderbilt Whitney 31.187

Early Morning, Grande Bleue
1929, watercolor and ink on paper,
10 x 14 inches
signed and dated at lower left: Guy Pène du Bois Nice 1929
titled at lower center: Early Morning Grande Bleue

The Detroit Institute of Arts; Founders Society Purchase, Merrill Fund

Sketch for Grande Bleue, Nice
1930, pencil on paper
5¼ x 8⅛ inches
Signed at lower right: Guy Pène du Bois

Private collection

Sketch for Grande Bleue, Nice
1930, pencil on paper
5¼ x 8⅛ inches
Signed at lower right: Guy Pène du Bois

Private collection

Grande Bleue, Nice | 1930, oil on canvas, 29 x 36 inches | signed and dated at lower left: Guy Pène du Bois '30

Private collection

Sketch for Place Massena, Nice
1930, pencil on paper, 8⅛ x 5¼ inches
unsigned

Private collection

Sketch for Place Massena, Nice
1930, pencil on paper, 5¼ x 8⅛ inches
unsigned

Private collection

123

Place Massena, Nice | 1930, oil on canvas, 29 x 36 inches | signed and dated at lower left: Guy Pène du Bois 30

Private collection

Sketch for Promenade

1930, pencil on paper, 8⅛ x 5¼ inches
unsigned

Private collection

124

125

Promenade | 1930, oil on canvas, 36½ x 29½ inches | signed and dated at lower right: Guy Pène du Boi / 30

Indianapolis Museum of Art, James E. Roberts Fund

Soldiers | 1930, oil on canvas, 21¾ x 18 inches | signed at lower right: Guy Pène du Bois (illeg.)

Hirshhorn Museum and Sculpture Garden, Smithsonian Institution, Washington, D.C.; Gift of Joseph H. Hirshhorn, 1966

Blue Shoe Shop | 1931, oil on canvas, 25 x 20 inches | signed lower right: Guy Pène du Bois

Naples Museum of Art, Florida, 2000.15.171; endowed by William J. and Suzanne V. von Liebig

Rose Madder Club | 1934, oil on canvas, 25 x 36 inches | unsigned

Archive photograph courtesy of the Estate of Yvonne Pène du Bois McKenney

Jane, ca. 1935, oil on canvas, 30 x 25 inches | signed at lower right: Guy Pène du Bois

The Estate of Yvonne Pène du Bois McKenney and James Graham & Sons, Inc., New York

Hostess | 1935–39, oil on canvas, 20 x 16 inches | signed at lower right: Guy Pène du Bois

Private collection

133

Portrait of Yvonne | ca. 1935, oil on canvas, 38 x 29 inches | signed at lower left: Guy Pène du Bois

The Park (Picnic Staten Island) | 1935, oil on canvas, 29 x 36 inches

Archive photograph courtesy of the Estate of Yvonne Pène du Bois McKenney and James Graham & Sons, Inc., New York

The Battery/Seaport | 1936, oil on canvas, 63 x 45 inches | signed and dated at lower right: Guy Pène du Bois 36

Private collection

Sketch for Girls Against the Sky

1937, pencil and crayon on paper, 10¼ x 16½ inches

signed at lower right center: G P. du Bois

Private collection

Girls Against the Sky | 1937, oil on canvas, 39 9/16 x 60¼ inches | signed and dated at lower right: Guy Pène du Bois/1937

Naples Museum of Art, Florida, 2000.15.167; Endowed by William J. and Suzanne V. von Liebig

Watching the Fleet | 1938, oil on canvas, 24 x 34 inches | signed and dated at lower right: Guy Pène du Bois '38

Vance Jordan Fine Art, New York

Long Island Beach | 1939, oil on canvas, 16 x 20 inches | signed and dated at lower right: Guy Pène du Bois / '39

Private collection

Along the River/Staten Island Outing | 1939, oil on canvas, 25 x 30 inches | signed and dated at lower left: Guy Pène du Bois 39

Archive photograph courtesy of the Estate of Yvonne Pène du Bois McKenney

Shopper in a Red Hat | 1939, oil on canvas, 30 x 25 inches | signed and dated at lower right: Guy Pène du Bois '39

Hunter Museum of American Art, Chattanooga, Tennessee; Gift of the Benwood Foundation

Waiting/Three Girls on the Staten Island Ferry | 1939, oil on canvas, 20 x 16 inches | signed and dated at lower right: Guy Pène du Bois 39

Private collection

OPPOSITE: **Portrait of Portia Lebrun** | 1939, oil on canvas, 71½ x 39 inches | signed and dated at lower right: Guy Pène du Bois 39

Private collection

Portrait of Portia Lebrun in a Pink Blouse | 1942, oil on canvas, 40 x 30 inches | signed and dated at lower left: Guy Pène du Bois '42

Indianapolis Museum of Art, Gift of Mrs. Booth Tarkington

Peruvian Indian | 1941, oil on canvas, 35 x 24 inches | signed and dated at lower right: Guy Pène du Bois '41

The Estate of Yvonne Pène du Bois McKenney and James Graham & Sons, Inc., New York

Wartime Cocktail | 1945, oil on canvas, 30 x 20 inches | signed at lower right: Guy Pène du Bois

Private collection

The Ace of Spades | 1945, oil on canvas, 18¼ x 24¼ inches | signed at lower left: Guy Pène du Bois

Private collection

The Puritan | ca. 1945, oil on canvas, 18 x 22 inches | signed at lower right: Guy Pène du Bois

Archive photograph courtesy of the Estate of Yvonne Pène du Bois McKenney

Two Figures in Courtroom | ca. 1945, oil on paper, mounted on artist board, 16 x 22¼ inches | unsigned

James Graham & Sons, Inc., New York

The Beauty | ca. 1946, oil on canvas, 29¾ x 24¼ inches | signed at lower left: Guy Pène du Bois

Archive photograph courtesy of the Estate of Yvonne Pène du Bois McKenney

Dramatic Moment | 1946, oil on canvas, 30 x 25 inches | signed at lower right: Guy Pène du Bois

Archive photograph courtesy of the Estate of Yvonne Pène du Bois McKenney

Addressing the Jury | 1947, oil on masonite, 19⅝ x 25½ inches | signed and dated at lower right: Guy Pène du Bois '47

SBC Communications Inc., San Antonio, Texas

Another Expulsion | 1950, oil on canvas, 40 x 30 inches | signed at lower right: Guy Pène du Bois

The Estate of Yvonne Pène du Bois McKenney and James Graham & Sons, Inc., New York

159

Café de Flore | 1954, oil on canvas, 15 x 24 inches | signed and dated at lower right: Guy Pène du Bois/1954

Private collection

Chronology

Throughout his career, Guy Pène du Bois participated in major group exhibitions, often large annuals or biennials, of contemporary American art. Some of these have been indicated in the chronology.

1884

4 January, is born in Brooklyn, New York, the son of Henri (1859–1906) and Laura Hague Pène du Bois. He is named after Guy de Maupassant, a friend of his father's.

1898

His family moves to Staten Island.

1899–1905

Studies at the New York School of Art; his teachers include William Merritt Chase, James Carroll Beckwith, Frank Vincent Du Mond, and Kenneth Hayes Miller.

1902

Begins study with Robert Henri, who is hired that year, and becomes class monitor. Fellow students include Edward Hopper, Clarence K. Chatterton, Arthur E. Cedarquist, Glenn O. Coleman, Rockwell Kent, Gifford Beal, George Bellows, Homer Boss, Patrick Henry Bruce, Oliver N. Chaffee, Lawrence T. Dresser, Arnold Friedman, Julius Golz, Jr., Prosper Invernizzi, Edward R. Keefe, John Koopman, Vachel Lindsay, Walter Pach, Eugene Speicher, Carl Sprinchorn, Walter Tittle, Walter Biggs, and Clifton Webb. Makes first sale, a portrait of a Staten Islander.

1905

April, sails for Europe with father. After several weeks in London, they settle in Paris. Studies at the Atelier Colarossi and takes private lessons from Théophile Steinlen. Makes exhibition debut at the Paris Salon.

1906

May, father falls ill in Gibraltar. July, sails for New York; father dies of heart disease at sea at the age of forty-seven. 21 July, arrives back in New York. August, begins work as a general reporter for the *New York American* and later is made music critic. Takes studio on West 23rd Street. Group exhibition: Pennsylvania Academy of the Fine Arts.

1907

Group exhibition: Gallery of the New York School of Art.

1908

December, first art criticism published in the *New York American*. Group exhibition: 9–31 March, "Exhibition of Paintings and Drawings by Contemporary American Artists," Old Harmonie Club, 43–45 West 42nd Street. Organized by Arnold Friedman, Julius Golz, Jr., and Glenn O. Coleman, with paintings by Pène du Bois, Edward Hopper, George Bellows, Lawrence T. Dresser, Edward R. Keefe, Rockwell Kent, George McKay, Howard McLean, Carl Sprinchorn, and C. Leroy Williams. Pène du Bois exhibited *Gaité Montparnasse*. Included in first Independents Show, New York.

1909

Becomes full-time art critic for the *New York American*.

1910

Group exhibition: The Independents.

1911

10 April, marries Florence ("Floy") Sherman Duncan on Staten Island. December, first article published in *Arts and Decoration*. Group exhibition: The Independents.

1912

May, leaves the *New York American*. Joins the Association of American Painters and Sculptors (AAPS). Group exhibition: "Exhibition of Paintings,"

The MacDowell Club of New York, 108 West 55th Street, with paintings by Pène du Bois, Edward Hopper, George Bellows, Randall Davey, Leon Kroll, Mountfort Coolidge, Rufus J. Dryer, and May Wilson Preston (22 February–5 March).

1913
Serves on publicity committee for the Armory Show and edits special issue of *Arts and Decoration*. Resigns from AAPS. 3 July, daughter, Yvonne, born. Kraushaar Galleries begins to handle work. Mother dies. Appointed editor of *Arts and Decoration*, replacing Hamilton Easter Field. Group exhibition: Armory Show (*"Waiter!"*; *Interior*; *Twentieth-Century Youth*; *Cascade, Bois de Boulogne*; *Virginia*; and *The Politician*).

1913–1914
Assistant to Royal Cortissoz at the *New York Tribune*.

1914
April, moves to Nutley, New Jersey. Group exhibitions: Montross Gallery, New York (shows four works, Bellows and Hopper also included); Corcoran.

1915
Group exhibitions: Montross Gallery, New York; Panama-Pacific International Exposition, San Francisco, California.

1916
9 May, son, William, born. June, loses job at *Arts and Decoration*, but hired back as editor by new owner. Takes job as art critic for the *New York Post*. Group exhibitions: Corcoran, Daniel Gallery, Montross Gallery, New York.

1917
Moves back to New York City. First Whitney Studio show. Becomes editor of *Arts and Decoration*. October, replaces Forbes Watson at the *New York Post*. Group exhibitions: Buffalo, Daniel Gallery, Montross Gallery, New York, Pennsylvania Academy of the Fine Arts, Whitney Studio.

1918
April, leaves job as art critic for the *New York Post*. Helps organize American Artists Mutual Aid Society to help artists hurt by war. Spring, charter member, Whitney Studio Club. November, has first solo exhibition at the Whitney Studio Club. Group exhibitions: Bourgeois Gallery, Buffalo, Kraushaar Galleries, Montross Gallery, New York, Pennsylvania Academy of the Fine Arts, Whitney Studio.

1919
Summer, visits Monhegan Island, Maine, with Hopper, Chatterton, and Floy. August, solo exhibition: Newport Art Association, Newport, Rhode Island. Group exhibitions: Buffalo, Dallas, St. Louis, Wildenstein.

1920
Arranges for first solo show of Edward Hopper at the Whitney Studio Club. Moves to Westport, Connecticut. Group exhibitions: Detroit Institute of Arts, Folsom Gallery, Kraushaar Galleries, Venice Biennale, Wildenstein.

1921
Leaves *Arts and Decoration* for good. Juror, 8th Exhibition of Oil Paintings by Contemporary American Artists, Corcoran Gallery of Art. Group exhibitions: Art Institute of Chicago, Buffalo, Corcoran, Dallas, Folsom Gallery, Kraushaar, Wildenstein, Whitney Studio Club.

1920–1924
Teaches at Art Students League (head and figure). Students include Alexander Calder, Isabel Bishop, Jack Tworkov, and Raphael Soyer.

1922

Writes "Art by the Way" for *International Studio*.
4–30 April, first solo exhibition at Kraushaar Galleries.
Group exhibitions: Art Institute of Chicago, Buffalo,
Dallas, Kraushaar, Whitney Studio Club.

1923

Teaches private painting and drawing class in New
York studio. First new issue of *Arts* appears under the
editorship of Forbes Watson; Pène du Bois a frequent
contributor until it ceases publication in 1931. Group
exhibitions: Buffalo, Carnegie, Cleveland, New Society
of Artists, New York, Whitney Studio Club.

1924

9 July, Edward Hopper and Josephine Nivison
married, New York; Pène du Bois best man.
Visits Hoppers in Gloucester during the summer.
December, sells house in Westport and leaves for
France. Settles first in Paris, then moves to Garnes,
about forty kilometers from Paris. Solo exhibi-
tion: Kraushaar Galleries (17 March–2 April).
Group exhibitions: Art Institute of Chicago, Buffalo,
Carnegie, Cincinnati, Cleveland, Kraushaar, New
Society of Artists, New York, Pennsylvania Academy
of the Fine Arts, Rochester.

1925

Shops wins third prize at the First Pan-American
Exhibition of Oil Paintings, Los Angeles County
Museum. Solo exhibition: Kraushaar Galleries
(3–15 November). Group exhibitions: Art Institute
of Chicago, Buffalo, Carnegie, Cleveland, Detroit
Institute of Arts, New Society of Artists, New York,
Pennsylvania Academy of the Fine Arts, Rochester.

1926

Attends gala dedication of Gertrude Vanderbilt
Whitney's monument at St. Nazaire, France, commem-
orating the spot where the first contingent of the
American Expeditionary Force landed in 1917. Group
exhibitions: Cleveland, Pennsylvania Academy of the
Fine Arts, Whitney Studio Club, Buffalo, Art Institute
of Chicago, Cleveland, New Society of Artists, New
York, Kraushaar, San Francisco.

1927

In Italy for six weeks to paint a portrait of Mrs. Charles
Bedaux at her villa near Florence. Solo exhibition:
Kraushaar Galleries (6–28 December). Group exhibi-
tions: Denver, Detroit Institute of Arts, Buffalo,
Cleveland, Minneapolis, National Academy of Design,
Pennsylvania Academy of the Fine Arts, San Francisco,
Wildenstein, Whitney Studio Club.

1928

September and October, visits Italy, stopping in Rome
and Anticoli. Solo exhibition: Kraushaar Galleries
(27 December–27 January 1929). Group exhibitions: Art Institute of Chicago, Brooklyn, Carnegie,
Cleveland, Corcoran, Detroit Institute of Arts,
Pennsylvania Academy of the Fine Arts, Phillips,
Toledo, Whitney Studio Club.

1929

March–October, in United States. Member, American
Jury of Selection, International Exhibition of Painting,
Carnegie Institute. Moves to Nice, where he hears
of stock market crash. Attends dedication of Gertrude
Vanderbilt Whitney's Columbus monument in
Palos, Spain. Solo exhibition: Kraushaar Galleries
(4–16 February). Group exhibitions: Art Institute
of Chicago, Carnegie, Cincinnati, Cleveland,
Pennsylvania Academy of the Fine Arts, Toledo,
Whitney Studio Club.

1930

April, returns to New York. Wins All-American Nineteen Contest from *Arts*. *Valley of the Chevreuse* wins Norman Wait Harris Prize, 43rd Annual Exhibit of American Painting and Sculpture, Art Institute of Chicago. Juror, 12th Exhibition of Contemporary American Oil Painting, Corcoran Gallery of Art. Solo exhibition: Kraushaar Galleries (26 February – 15 March). Group exhibitions: Art Institute of Chicago, Buffalo, Carnegie, Cincinnati, Cleveland, Corcoran, Los Angeles County Museum of Art, Museum of Modern Art, Pennsylvania Academy of the Fine Arts, St. Louis.

1930 – 1932

Teaches at Art Students League (life drawing, painting and composition, illustration).

1931

November, Juror, Art Institute of Chicago. Whitney Museum of American Art opens in November and Pène du Bois one of many artists represented in the inaugural exhibition. Royal Cortissoz publishes a monograph on Pène du Bois as part of the Whitney's American Artists Series. Group exhibitions: Art Institute of Chicago, Baltimore, Brooklyn, Buffalo, Carnegie, Cincinnati, Cleveland, Kraushaar, Pennsylvania Academy of the Fine Arts.

1932

January, launches Guy Pène du Bois School. Made an Associate of *Arts Weekly*. Begins teaching summer school in Stonington, Connecticut. Solo exhibition: Kraushaar Galleries (29 March – 19 April). Group exhibitions: Art Institute of Chicago, Cleveland, Corcoran, Milwaukee, National Academy of Design, Pennsylvania Academy of the Fine Arts, Rhode Island School of Design, St. Louis, Whitney.

1933

Group exhibitions: Art Institute of Chicago, Carnegie, Cleveland, Kansas City, Kraushaar, Pennsylvania Academy of the Fine Arts.

1934

Paints Jumble Shop Restaurant murals. Group exhibitions: Art Institute of Chicago, Carnegie, Cleveland, Kansas City, Pennsylvania Academy of the Fine Arts, Springfield, Venice Biennale, Whitney.

1935

Solo exhibition: Kraushaar Galleries (16 January – 2 February). Group exhibitions: Art Institute of Chicago, Brooklyn, Carnegie, Cleveland, Corcoran, National Academy of Design, Rhode Island School of Design, San Francisco, Toledo, Worcester.

1935 – 1936

Teaches at Art Students League (life drawing, painting, and composition).

1936

Carnival Interlude wins Second Altman Prize, 11th Annual Exhibition, National Academy of Design. Juror, 34th International, Carnegie Institute. Enters Justice Department mural competition; selected for special consideration for a commission elsewhere. Paints mural, *Saratoga in the Racing Season*, for post office, Saratoga Springs, New York, sponsored by the Treasury Art Relief Project (TRAP). August, daughter Yvonne marries Houghton Field Furlong in August 1936 (they separate by the end of World War II). Solo exhibition: Kraushaar Galleries (11 – 28 November). Group exhibitions: Art Institute of Chicago, Brooklyn, Buffalo, Carnegie, Cleveland, Kraushaar, National Academy of Design, Pennsylvania Academy of the Fine Arts, Whitney.

1937

Meditation wins Second William A. Clark Prize, and Corcoran Silver Medal, 15th Biennial Exhibition of Contemporary American Oil Paintings, Corcoran Gallery of Art. Elected Associate Member, National Academy of Design. Paints mural, *John Jay at His Home*, for post office in Rye, New York. Group exhibitions: Carnegie, Cincinnati, Corcoran, National Academy of Design, Pennsylvania Academy of the Fine Arts, Rhode Island School of Design, Whitney.

1938

Solo exhibition: Kraushaar Galleries (15 November– 10 December). Group exhibitions: Art Institute of Chicago, Cincinnati, Kraushaar, National Academy of Design, Pennsylvania Academy of the Fine Arts, Whitney.

1938–1939

Summer, teaches at Hilton Leach's Amagansett Art School, Long Island.

1939

Member, Painters' Jury of Selection, 134th Annual Exhibition of Painting and Sculpture, Pennsylvania Academy of the Fine Arts. Teaches at the Cooper Union School of Art. Moves into house at 20 West 10th Street, where he lives for the remainder of his New York years. Solo exhibitions: Carnegie Institute (4–22 January), Corcoran Gallery of Art (18 November–15 December). Group exhibitions: Art Institute of Chicago, Corcoran, Carnegie, Kraushaar, National Academy of Design, Pennsylvania Academy of the Fine Arts, San Francisco, Whitney.

1940

Artists Say the Silliest Things published by the American Artists Group. Jury of Selection, 114th Annual Exhibition, National Academy of Design. Elected Life Member of the Lotos Club. Elected full Academician, National Academy of Design. Suffers heart attack at his summer school in Stonington, Connecticut.

Solo exhibition: Washington County Museum of Fine Arts, Hagerstown, Maryland (1–25 January); this show traveled to the Mint Museum of Art, Charlotte, North Carolina (February) and to the Museum of Arts and Sciences in Norfolk, Virginia (March). Group exhibitions: Carnegie, Cincinnati, National Academy of Design, Pennsylvania Academy of the Fine Arts, Rhode Island School of Design, San Francisco, St. Louis, Whitney.

1941

Suffers second heart attack. Juror, 17th Biennial Exhibition of Contemporary American Oil Paintings, Corcoran Gallery of Art. Elected to the Department of Art, National Institute of Arts and Letters. Group exhibitions: Art Institute of Chicago, Cincinnati, Corcoran, Kraushaar, Pennsylvania Academy of the Fine Arts, Whitney.

1942

20 April, honorary pallbearer at funeral of Gertrude Vanderbilt Whitney, with Hopper, Eugene Speicher, John Carroll, and eight others. Jury of Selection, 116th Annual Exhibition of Contemporary American Painting and Sculpture, National Academy of Design. *Old Trouper* wins Maynard Prize, Museum of Fine Arts, Boston. Paints mural, *The Landing of the Weston Company*, for the Weymouth branch of the Boston post office. Solo exhibition: Kraushaar Galleries (26 January–21 February). Group exhibitions: Art Institute of Chicago, Kraushaar, National Academy of Design, Pennsylvania Academy of the Fine Arts, Whitney.

1942–1944

Member, advisory council, Cooper Union.

1943

Summer, move into house on Farmholme Road, Stonington, Connecticut. Solo exhibition: Kraushaar Galleries (24 November–18 December). Group exhibitions: Art Institute of Chicago, Carnegie, Corcoran,

Kraushaar, Pennsylvania Academy of the Fine Arts,
San Francisco, Whitney.

1944

Elected to board of Audubon Artists. Group exhibitions: Cincinnati, Kraushaar, Pennsylvania Academy of the Fine Arts, St. Louis, Whitney.

1945

Juror, 35th Annual Exhibition of Associated Artists of Pittsburgh. *Cocktails* wins First Altman Prize, National Academy of Design. Initiating Sponsor, Independent Citizens' Committee of the Arts, Sciences and Professions. Group exhibitions: Carnegie, Cleveland, Corcoran, National Academy of Design, Los Angeles County Museum of Art, Pennsylvania Academy of the Fine Arts, Whitney.

1946

Cocktails purchased by the George A. Hearn Fund for The Metropolitan Museum of Art. *After Dinner Speaker* wins prize at Salmagundi Club's Second Annual Exhibition of Paintings. John Kraushaar dies. March–April, visits New Orleans. Is included in "Robert Henri and Five of His Pupils," an exhibition organized by Helen Appleton Read at the Century Association; George Bellows, Eugene Speicher, Rockwell Kent, and Edward Hopper also included. Solo exhibition: Kraushaar Galleries (18 November–7 December). Group exhibitions: Pennsylvania Academy of the Fine Arts, Whitney.

1947

May, breaks with Kraushaar Galleries. Group exhibitions: Cleveland, Corcoran, National Academy of Design, Pennsylvania Academy of the Fine Arts, Whitney.

1948

Juliana Force dies. Group exhibitions: Pennsylvania Academy of the Fine Arts, Whitney.

1949

March, Floy suffers a stroke. December, Guy is hospitalized with first symptoms of cancer. Group exhibitions: National Academy of Design, Pennsylvania Academy of the Fine Arts, Whitney.

1950

Guy hospitalized. 10 September, Floy dies. Group exhibitions: Carnegie, National Academy of Design, Whitney.

1951

Group exhibitions: Corcoran, National Academy of Design, Whitney.

1952

Group exhibition: Whitney.

1953

Becomes involved in *Reality: A Journal of Artists' Opinions* with Edward Hopper, Isabel Bishop, Raphael Soyer, and other realist artists.

1953

March, after a studio sale, leaves with Yvonne for Paris. July, suffers another heart attack.

1954

Paints last dated canvas, *Café de Flore*. Yvonne divorced from Houghton Furlong. Solo exhibition: Staten Island Museum (14 November–14 December).

1956

Suffers another heart attack. December, Guy and Yvonne return to the United States. Yvonne marries James Harvey McKenney, and Guy settles with them in Boston.

1957

Group exhibitions: Corcoran, Kraushaar, Toledo.

1958

18 July, dies in Boston.

165

Endnotes

1. Mahonri Young, "Guy Pène du Bois," review of a show at Kraushaar Galleries, 1921, otherwise unidentified clipping, vertical files, Corcoran Gallery of Art, Washington, D.C.

2. Ibid.

3. Duncan Phillips, *A Collection in the Making*, Phillips Publications, no. 5 (New York: E. Weyhe, 1926), 70.

4. Shamim Momin, "Artists of Modern Life: Baudelaire in the New World," in *Talk of the Town: Guy Pène du Bois and Elie Nadelman*, exh. cat. (Stamford, Conn.: Whitney Museum of American Art at Champion, 2000), 3.

5. Homer Saint-Gaudens, *The American Artist and His Times* (New York: Dodd, Mead, 1941), 284.

6. Pène du Bois's other professors included James Carroll Beckwith, Frank Vincent Du Mond, and Kenneth Hayes Miller. The tired academicism of the first two and the aridly rigid Renaissance realism of the third exerted little influence on his work.

7. Guy Pène du Bois, *Artists Say the Silliest Things* (New York: American Artists Group, 1940), 86.

8. Guy Pène du Bois, "Who's Who in American Art," *Arts and Decoration* 6 (November 1915): 33.

9. Helen Appleton Read, *Robert Henri*, American Artists Series (New York: Whitney Museum of American Art, 1931), 10.

10. Robert Henri, quoted in Forbes Watson, "Robert Henri," *The Arts* 16 (September 1929): 3.

11. Ibid.

12. Guy Pène du Bois to Robert Henri, 22 September 1920, Robert Henri Papers, mss 100, box 3, folder 77, Yale Collection of American Literature, Beinecke Library, Yale University, New Haven, Connecticut.

13. This work was once in the collection of writer Van Wyck Brooks, a Westport neighbor, who probably bought it about the time he went to France, in 1924.

14. Marsden Hartley, *Adventures in the Arts* (New York: Boni and Liveright, 1921), 197.

15. Guy Pène du Bois to Robert Henri, 23 November 1905, Henri Papers. He also wrote: "If you go to the Pennsylvania Academy will you please look for my picture *Wrestlers at Neuilly* and write me what you think about it and how it is hung? I sent three and had only this one accepted."

The painting to which he refers was once identified as having been done on Staten Island, but his letter clearly shows it was done in France and shipped back home for exhibition. The Henri painting to which he refers is *La Neige (The Snow)* which had been purchased by the Luxembourg in 1899.

16. Guy Pène du Bois to Robert Henri, 17 February 1906, Henri Papers.

17. Pène du Bois, *Artists Say the Silliest Things*, 110.

18. The artist was not consistent in this practice, however. Although he promised to sign his work "Guy Pène du Bois," in correspondence he often signed his name "Guy du Bois." He alternates between "du Bois" and "Pène du Bois" in his correspondence with Kraushaar in the 1920s, and as late as 1953 uses "du Bois," the name by which most artists referred to him.

19. Pène du Bois, *Artists Say the Silliest Things*, 128.

20. Pène du Bois, *Artists Say the Silliest Things*, 132.

21. The artist's wife made her debut as a concert pianist in Chicago in 1894. While she ultimately decided not to pursue a professional career, she played the piano for the rest of her life and was friends with Arthur Rubinstein. *Artist's Wife, No. 2* (1926, Chrysler Museum) shows her at an upright piano.

22. Guy Pène du Bois, Diary, 12 April 1919, Guy Pène du Bois Papers, Archives of American Art/Smithsonian Institution.

23. Guy Pène du Bois, "Guy Pène du Bois by Guy Pène du Bois," *International Studio* 75 (June 1922): 243.

24. Guy Pène du Bois, "Honoré Daumier," in *Honoré Daumier: Appreciations of His Life and Works*, Phillips Publications, no. 2 (New York: E. P. Dutton, 1922), 49.

25. Guy Pène du Bois, "The Spirit and Chronology of the Modern Movement," *Arts and Decoration* 3 (March 1913): 178.

26. Guy Pène du Bois, "Caricatures are Difficult to Draw, Because They Must Be Devoid of All Malice," *New York American*, 8 August 1910.

27. Pène du Bois, Diary, 15 October 1913.

28. Lewis A. Erenberg, *Steppin' Out: New York Nightlife and the Transformation of American Culture, 1890–1930* (Westport, Conn.: Greenwood Press, 1981), table 1.

29. Pène du Bois quoted in Catherine Beach Ely, *The Modern Tendency in American Painting* (New York: Frederick Fairchild Sherman, 1925), 75.

30. Pène du Bois, Diary, 7 October 1917.

31. *Intellect and Intuition* was once owned by Mary Harriman Rumsey, the wife of sculptor Cary Rumsey. She was the daughter of railroad magnate Edward Henry

Harriman and Mary Williamson Averell Harriman and lived on the family estate at Arden, New York. Guy wrote on her collection and that of her mother.

32. Pène du Bois, *Artists Say the Silliest Things,* 191.

33. Pène du Bois, Diary, 5 October 1913.

34. For more on Laporte, see "Collection of Mr. and Mrs. William F. Laporte, Passaic, N.J.," in *French, American, and Other Modern Paintings, Bronzes,* sale no. 550 (New York: Sotheby Parke-Bernet, 30 March 1944). For more on Egner, see "Collection of the Late Arthur F. Egner, South Orange, New Jersey," in Paintings by Contemporary Artists of American and Other Schools, sale no. 670 (New York: Sotheby Parke-Bernet, 4 May 1945,); and Guy Pène du Bois, "The Collection of Mr. Arthur Egner," *Arts and Decoration* 7 (August 1917): 475–78.

35. Pène du Bois, Diary, 3 May 1924.

36. William B. McCormick, "Guy Pène du Bois — Social Historian," *Arts and Decoration* 4 (November 1913): 16.

37. Duncan Phillips to Guy Pène du Bois, 12 April 1923, quoted in Erika D. Passantino, ed., *The Eye of Duncan Phillips: A Collection in the Making* (Washington, D.C.: The Phillips Collection, in association with Yale University Press, 1999), 370 (entry by Virginia Speer Burden).

38. Guy Pène du Bois, "Robert Winthrop Chanler: The Man, A Normal Exotic," *Arts and Decoration* 14 (January 1921): 192.

39. Pène du Bois, *Artists Say the Silliest Things,* 176.

40. James Charters, *Hemingway's Paris,* as told to Morrill Cody (1934; New York: Tower, 1965), 95.

41. Pène du Bois, Diary, 22 May 1921.

42. Ibid., 25 October 1924.

43. Pène du Bois, *Artists Say the Silliest Things,* 214.

44. Ibid.

45. Guy Pène du Bois to John Kraushaar, 23 November 1926, Kraushaar Papers, Archives of American Art/Smithsonian Institution.

46. Ibid., 1 December 1926.

47. Ibid.

48. *Blue Armchair* (1923, Phillips Collection) depicts Neely McCoy, who was the wife of his good friend Samuel Duff McCoy. When he painted Neely in Westport during the summer of 1923 she was about thirty-eight years old, and she and the artist had an affair. See Burden entry in Passantino, *The Eye of Duncan Phillips,* 371. His portrait *Mary at the Garden Entrance* (1928, unlocated) depicts sculptor Mary Lightfoot Tarleton Knollenberg. She was pursued romantically by Mahonri Young and later by Pène du Bois. See Norma S. Davis, *A Song of Joys: The Biography of Mahonri Mackintosh Young, Sculptor, Painter, Etcher* (Provo, Utah: Brigham Young University Museum of Art, 1999).

49. Pène du Bois, Diary, 6 April 1924.

50. Guy Pène du Bois to John Kraushaar, [June] 1926, Kraushaar Papers.

51. William Glackens to Edith Glackens, 8 May 1928, quoted in Ira Glackens, *William Glackens and The Eight: The Artists Who Freed American Art,* rev. ed. (New York: Writers and Readers Publishing, 1990), 222.

52. Pène du Bois, Diary, 22 March 1926.

53. Guy Pène du Bois to John Kraushaar, 23 November 1926, Kraushaar Papers.

54. Ibid., 24 March 1925.

55. Ibid., 24 October 1925.

56. Ibid., 17 May 1927.

57. Ibid., 17 December 1928.

58. John Kraushaar to Guy Pène du Bois, 16 April 1926, Kraushaar Papers.

59. Guy Pène du Bois to John Kraushaar, 12 March 1925, Kraushaar Papers.

60. John Kraushaar to Guy Pène du Bois, 9 October 1926, Kraushaar Papers.

61. Guy Pène du Bois to John Kraushaar, 24 October 1926, Kraushaar Papers.

62. Yvonne Pène du Bois McKenney, unpublished biography of Guy Pène du Bois, ca. 1963, Pène du Bois Papers.

63. Guy Pène du Bois to John Kraushaar, 6 March 1925, Kraushaar Papers.

64. Ibid., 6 April 1925.

65. Ibid.

66. Ibid., 2 March 1925.

67. Ibid., 20 October 1927.

68. John Kraushaar to Guy Pène du Bois, 7 December 1928, Kraushaar Papers.

69. Pène du Bois, Diary, 5 October 1913.

70. Guy Pène du Bois to John Kraushaar, 30 July 1925, Kraushaar Papers.

71. Ibid., 14 August 1925.

72. Ibid., 28 September 1928.

73. John Kraushaar to Guy Pène du Bois, 15 October 1928, Kraushaar Papers.

74. Ibid., 10 November 1928.

75. Guy Pène du Bois to John Kraushaar, 20 October 1928, Kraushaar Papers.

76. Ibid., 2 November 1928.

77. Ibid., 28 December 1928.

78. John Kraushaar to Guy Pène du Bois, 26 January 1926, Kraushaar Papers.

79. Ibid.

80. Ibid., 5 March 1926.

81. Ibid., 16 April 1926.

82. Ibid., 10 May 1926.

83. Ibid., 26 August 1926.

84. Ibid., 15 December 1926.

85. Ibid., 29 April 1927.

86. Ibid., 3 October 1927.

87. Ibid.

88. Guy Pène du Bois to John Kraushaar, 20 October 1928, Kraushaar Papers.

89. John Kraushaar to Guy Pène du Bois, 6 February 1929, Kraushaar Papers.

90. Guy Pène du Bois to John Kraushaar, 11 February 1929, Kraushaar Papers.

91. John Kraushaar to Guy Pène du Bois, 9 March 1929, Kraushaar Papers.

92. Henry McBride, "Expatriate Artists Are Finding the Going Increasingly Rough," *New York Sun*, 9 February 1929.

93. John Kraushaar to Guy Pène du Bois, 10 May 1926, Kraushaar Papers.

94. Guy Pène du Bois to John Kraushaar, [June] 1926, Kraushaar Papers.

95. Al Laney, *Paris* Herald: *The Incredible Newspaper* (New York: D. Appleton-Century, 1947), 3. The author had been in Paris during the twenties.

96. Helen Henderson, "Viewing Work by Guy Pène du Bois," *Philadelphia Inquirer*, 6 November 1927.

97. Helen Appleton Read, "News and Views of Current Art: Guy Pène du Bois," *Brooklyn Daily Eagle*, 11 December 1927.

98. Stuart Preston, "New York: Guy Pène du Bois, Graham," *Burlington Magazine* 103 (June 1961): 293.

99. Read, "News and Views of Current Art."

100. Guy Pène du Bois to John Kraushaar, 4 March 1928, Kraushaar Papers.

101. Ibid., 2 July 1928.

102. For more on artistic depictions of women smoking in public, see Dolores Mitchell, "The 'New Woman' as Prometheus: Women Artists Depict Women Smoking," *Woman's Art Journal* 12, no. 1 (spring/summer 1991): 3–9.

103. Cited in Elizabeth Hutton Turner, *Americans in Paris (1921–1931): Man Ray, Gerald Murphy, Stuart Davis,* *Alexander Calder,* exh. cat. (Washington, D.C.: The Phillips Collection, 1996), 13.

104. Charters, *Hemingway's Paris,* 119.

105. Pène du Bois, Diary, 28 March 1929.

106. *Yvonne Pène du Bois: Paintings from the Last Four Decades* (New York: James Graham and Sons, 1985), 5.

107. For more on the Nice's popularity with artists, see Kenneth Wayne, John House, and Kenneth E. Silver, *Impressions of the Riviera: Monet, Renoir, Matisse, and Their Contemporaries,* exh. cat. (Portland, Me.: Portland Art Museum, 1998), and Kenneth E. Silver, *Making Paradise: Art, Modernity, and the Myth of the French Riviera* (Cambridge, Mass.: MIT Press, 2001).

108. John Kraushaar to Guy Pène du Bois, 9 January 1930, Kraushaar Papers.

109. Yvonne Pène du Bois McKenney, Memoirs, typescript, 225, Pène du Bois Papers.

110. John Kraushaar to Guy Pène du Bois, 15 August 1932, Kraushaar Papers.

111. Antoinette Kraushaar to Guy Pène du Bois, 24 July 1935, Kraushaar Papers.

112. Guy Pène du Bois, "A Modern American Collection: The Paintings of Contemporary Artists," *Arts and Decoration* 4 (June 1914): 325.

113. Edwin Alden Jewell, "Guy Pène du Bois's Show," *New York Times*, 14 November 1936.

114. Margaret Breuning, "The Whitney's Enlarged Annual," *Magazine of Art* 33 (February 1940): 100.

115. Glackens, *William Glackens and The Eight*, 236.

116. "That Damned Rose Madder Bunch," typescript, Pène du Bois Papers.

117. Guy Pène du Bois to Elizabeth Navas, 2 April 1940, quoted in George P. Tomko, *Catalogue of the Roland P. Murdock Collection* (Wichita: Wichita Art Museum, 1972), 52–53. See also Helen A. Harrison and Constance Ayers Denne, *Hamptons Bohemia: Two Centuries of Artists and Writers on the Beach* (San Francisco: Chronicle Books, 2002).

118. Poet Arthur Davison Ficke was a close friend of Edna St. Vincent Millay. He divorced his first wife in 1922 and married Gladys Brown in 1923. At some point the du Bois family purchased property from Ficke in Austerlitz, New York, next door to Millay's property; Guy sold it in 1951.

119. Edward B. Rowan to Guy Pène du Bois, 5 September 1936, Pène du Bois Papers.

120. Ibid.

121. This mural may also have been the result of the Justice competition, but the correspondence file relating to

it is missing from the National Archives. Other studies relating to it are reproduced in Edward Bruce and Forbes Watson, *Art in Federal Buildings: An Illustrated Record of the Treasury Department's New Program in Painting and Sculpture,* vol. 1, *Mural Designs, 1934–1936* (Washington, D.C.: Art in Federal Buildings, Inc., 1936), 264–66.

122. Saint-Gaudens, *American Artist and His Times,* 251.

123. Guy Pène du Bois to Edward B. Rowan, n.d. [between 8 and 19 January 1937]. All letters relating to Guy Pène du Bois's post office murals are at the National Archives and Records Administration (NARA), College Park, Maryland, Record Group 121, Records of the Public Buildings Service, Textual Records of the Section of Fine Arts, box 79, entry 133. Unless otherwise indicated, all archival references relating to these murals are from this source.

124. Ibid.

125. Edward B. Rowan to Guy Pène du Bois, 19 January 1937, NARA.

126. Guy Pène du Bois to Edward B. Rowan, 31 March 1937, NARA.

127. Ibid.

128. Ibid., 29 June 1937.

129. Ibid., 31 March 1937.

130. Edward B. Rowan to Guy Pène du Bois, 16 April 1937, NARA.

131. Ibid., 12 July 1937.

132. Ibid.

133. Guy Pène du Bois to Edward B. Rowan, 24 November 1937, NARA.

134. Ibid., 18 January 1938.

135. Ibid.

136. Ibid., 9 March 1938.

137. Ibid., 25 March 1942.

138. Edward B. Rowan to Guy Pène du Bois, 25 March 1942, NARA.

139. Edward B. Rowan to Postmaster, Weymouth Branch, 2 April 1942, NARA.

140. Guy Pène du Bois to Edward B. Rowan, 10 April 1942, NARA.

141. Ibid.

142. Ibid.

143. Ibid., 20 May 1942. The artist was to be paid $900 for the 5′8″ x 13′2″ mural. His contract was structured so he would receive $200 when the preliminary design was approved, $300 when a full-sized cartoon was approved, and the final $400 when the mural was installed and approved. He had eight months to finish it.

144. Ibid., 26 May 1942.

145. Ibid., 4 June 1942.

146. Ibid., 22 June 1942.

147. Pène du Bois, Diary, 16 September 1924.

148. Breuning, "Whitney's Enlarged Annual," 100.

149. Yvonne Pène du Bois McKenney to Virginia Speer Burden, 20 May 1991, quoted in Passantino, *Eye of Duncan Phillips,* 760, n. 10.

150. Guy Pène du Bois to Antoinette Kraushaar, 15 August 1941, Kraushaar Papers.

151. Guy Pène du Bois to Forbes Watson, 2 January 1942, Pène du Bois Papers.

152. Ibid.

153. Homer Saint-Gaudens to Guy Pène du Bois, 30 March 1942, Pène du Bois Papers.

154. Antoinette Kraushaar to Guy Pène du Bois, 14 May 1947, Kraushaar Papers.

155. "Their Summer Harvest," *Art Digest* 16 (1 October 1941): 19. When it was shown at Kraushaar in the summer of 1941 the work was titled *Peruvian Indian,* but at the earlier spring Corcoran Biennial it had appeared as *Chilean Indian.* In a 1945 auction, it was titled *Inca Model* (*Paintings of Various Schools,* sale no. 641 [New York: Sotheby Parke-Bernet, 28 February–1 March 1945], lot 18). More recently it has been titled *Inca Nude.*

156. Independent Citizens' Committee of the Arts, Sciences and Professions, By-laws, with Jo Davidson cover letter, 7 March 1945, Muriel Draper Papers, Yale Collection of American Literature, Beinecke Library, Yale University, New Haven, Connecticut.

157. Helen Appleton Read, *Robert Henri and Five of His Pupils,* exh. cat. (New York: Century Association, 1946), unpaged.

158. Pène du Bois, Diary, 2 December 1925.

159. Jo Hopper to Carl Sprinchorn, 20 September 1950, quoted in Gail Levin, *Edward Hopper: An Intimate Biography* (New York: Alfred A. Knopf, 1995), 431.

160. Pène du Bois, Diary, 27 October 1953.

161. Edward Hopper to Yvonne Pène du Bois McKenney, 21 July 1958, Pène du Bois Papers.

Selected Bibliography

Except for a few major sources, I have not duplicated the extensive bibliographies I compiled for the Corcoran (1980) and Sordoni (1995) catalogues listed below.

Published Sources

Berman, Avis. *Rebels on Eighth Street: Juliana Force and the Whitney Museum of American Art*. New York: Atheneum, 1990.

Cortissoz, Royal. *Guy Pène du Bois*. American Artists Series. New York: Whitney Museum of American Art, 1931.

Dawson, Anne E. *Idol of the Moderns: Pierre-Auguste Renoir and American Painting*. San Diego: San Diego Museum of Art, 2002.

Gerdts, William H., and Jorge H. Santis. *William Glackens*. Fort Lauderdale, Fla.: Museum of Art, in association with New York: Abbeville Press, 1996.

Fahlman, Betsy. "Guy Pène du Bois (1884–1958)," Ph.D. dissertation, University of Delaware, 1981.

————. *Guy Pène du Bois: Artist About Town*. Washington, D.C.: Corcoran Gallery of Art, 1980.

————. *Guy Pène du Bois (1884–1958): Returning to America*. New York: James Graham and Sons, 1998.

————. "Imaging the Twenties: The Work of Guy Pène du Bois," in *Guy Pène du Bois: The Twenties at Home and Abroad*. Wilkes-Barre, Pa.: Sordoni Gallery, Wilkes University, 1995.

Haskell, Barbara. *The American Century: Art and Culture, 1900–1950*. New York: Whitney Museum of American Art, 1999.

Hills, Patricia, and Roberta K. Tarbell. *The Figurative Tradition and the Whitney Museum of American Art: Paintings and Sculpture from the Permanent Collection*. New York: Whitney Museum of American Art, 1980.

Levin, Gail. *Edward Hopper: An Intimate Biography*. New York: Alfred A. Knopf, 1995.

Momin, Shamim. "Artists of Modern Life: Baudelaire in the New World," in *Talk of the Town: Guy Pène du Bois and Elie Nadelman*. Stamford, Conn.: Whitney Museum of American Art at Champion, 2000.

Park, Marlene, and Gerald E. Markowitz. *Democratic Vistas: Post Offices and Public Art in the New Deal*. Philadelphia: Temple University Press, 1984.

Passantino, Erika D., ed., *The Eye of Duncan Phillips: A Collection in the Making*. Washington, D.C.: The Phillips Collection in association with New Haven: Yale University Press, 1999.

Pène du Bois, Guy. *Artists Say the Silliest Things*. New York: American Artists Group, 1940.

Pisano, Ronald G. *Long Island Landscape Painting, Vol. II: The Twentieth Century*. Biographical essays by Beverly Rood. Boston: Little, Brown and Company, 1990.

Archival Sources

Guy Pène du Bois Papers, Archives of American Art, Smithsonian Institution, Washington, D.C.

Robert Henri Papers, Yale Collection of American Literature, Beinecke Library, Yale University, New Haven, Conn., MSS 100, box 3, folder 77.

Kraushaar Galleries Papers, Archives of American Art, Smithsonian Institution, Washington, D.C.

National Archives and Records Administration, College Park, Maryland, Record Group 121, Records of the Public Buildings Service, Textual Records of the Section of Fine Arts, box 79, entry 133.

Index

174